The Practical Encyclopedia of
EAST EUROPEAN COOKING

The Practical Encyclopedia of
EAST EUROPEAN
COOKING

The definitive collection of traditional recipes,
from the Baltic to the Black Sea

CONTRIBUTING EDITOR: LESLEY CHAMBERLAIN
RECIPE AUTHORS: CATHERINE ATKINSON AND TRISH DAVIES

LORENZ BOOKS

First published in 1999 by Lorenz Books

© Anness Publishing Limited 1999

Lorenz Books is an imprint of
Anness Publishing Limited
Hermes House
88–89 Blackfriars Road
London SE1 8HA

This edition published in Canada by Raincoast Books
8680 Cambie Street, Vancouver, British Columbia V6P 6M9

Published in the USA by Lorenz Books, Anness Publishing Inc.,
27 West 20th Street, New York, NY 10011; (800) 354-9657

ISBN 0 7548 0071 7

A CIP catalogue record for this book is available from the British Library

Publisher: Joanna Lorenz
Editor: Margaret Malone
Designer: Julie Francis
Jacket Designer: Mark Stevens
Copy Editor: Jo Lethaby
Photography: Dave Jordan and Ian Garlick
Food for Photography: Sara Lewis, assisted by Julie Beresford and
Clare Lewis, assisted by Sascha Brodie
Styling: Marion McLornan and Shannon Beare
Illustrators: Angela Wood (artworks) and David Cook (maps)
Editorial Reader: Joy Wotton
Production Controller: Julie Hadingham

Printed and bound in Singapore

1 3 5 7 9 10 8 6 4 2

Notes
For all recipes, quantities are given in both metric and imperial measures and, where appropriate,
measures are also given in standard cups and spoons.
Follow one set, but not a mixture, because they are not interchangeable.

Standard spoon and cup measures are level.
1 tsp = 5ml, 1 tbsp = 15ml, 1 cup = 250ml/8 fl oz

Australian standard tablespoons are 20ml. Australian readers should use 3 tsp in place of 1 tbsp
for measuring small quantities of gelatine, cornflour, salt, etc.

Size 3 (medium) eggs are used unless otherwise stated

CONTENTS

INTRODUCTION

From the Baltic Sea in the north to the Black Sea in the south, the cooking of Eastern Europe brings to mind hearty, flavoursome dishes. The product of a not always fruitful soil, everyday fare has been greatly influenced by the need to overcome long hard winters. The result, however, is wonderfully surprising. Though many common characteristics are shared, traditional food from Russia through to the Balkans can be surprisingly diverse and subtle in its ingenious use of ingredients and flavours.

Germans, Czechs, Hungarians, Poles, Ukrainians and Russians are all proud of their robust cuisines, which have changed little this century. Their repertoires include soups and stews of universal renown and the most nourishing bread to be found in the world. The cooking is long and slow, and the flavours, derived from vegetables and fish, are well developed.

While the southern cuisines of the Balkan countries of Romania, Bulgaria and former Yugoslavia share many flavours with their northern neighbours, the long hot summers and richer soil produce an enviable vegetable harvest. The region's dishes provide colourful contrasts to northern ones and are altogether spicier, with many flavours and textures influenced by Italy, Greece and Turkey.

It is no exaggeration therefore to say that the cooking of Eastern Europe takes in the flavours and traditions of half the world.

HISTORY AND REGIONAL CHARACTERISTICS

The great European empires played a major part in dividing this region, and this book, into three roughly geo-political areas: Russia, Ukraine and Poland; Germany, Austria, Hungary and the Czech Republic; the Balkans and the east Adriatic coast.

Eastern Europe is a major area on the food map. Russian cooking boasts rich sour soups, pancakes and porridges, and yeast-leavened baking. Central European cooking is the legacy of the Austro-Hungarian Empire with, as one of its jewels, its rich café culture. The cakes and pastries of Central Europe, such as *Linzertorte* and *Dobos Torta*, are world famous.

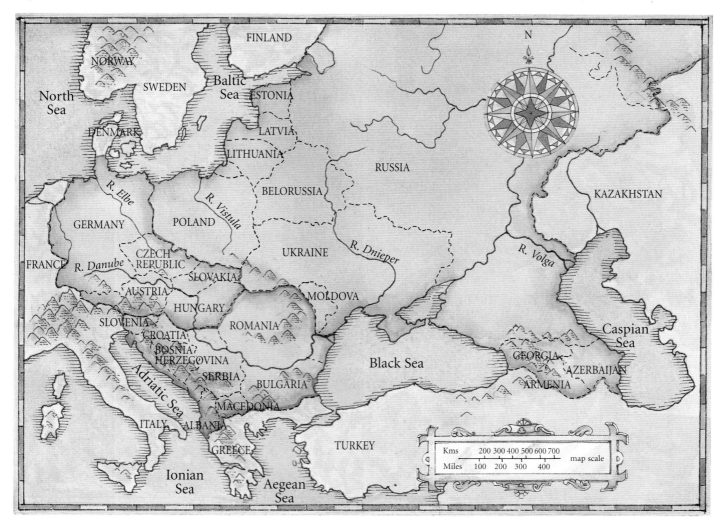

The spicier cooking of the Balkan countries, from Serbia in the west to Bulgaria in the east, and along the east Adriatic, comprises the third region, all of which was formerly part of the Ottoman Empire. These divisions, however, are not meant to be taken as fixed, and there is much movement between these three regions. The food of countries such as Hungary, Slovakia and Croatia, for example, draws on both Balkan and Central European influences, and German cooking provides the gateway to the rest of Europe.

FROM NORTH TO SOUTH

In north-east Europe, rye is the main cereal crop, rather than wheat, hence the customary black bread that has become a favourite around the world for its taste and nourishment. Typical vegetables from Germany to Russia are root crops: carrots, turnips, onions, potatoes, kohlrabi, beetroot and horseradish. Cabbages and flat leaf parsley are also universal, while the most common fruits are apples and summer berries. The north-east European diet has for centuries relied on preserved versions of these vegetables and fruits in winter. Hence, alongside pickled vegetables are high-quality jams, which are used for making excellent sweet pies and cakes. The tradition of annual jam-making is still widely practised in the home.

The northern half of Eastern Europe is also where the great mushrooming cultures have thrived, and a number of much-loved dishes, such as soups and stews, feature these miraculous fruits of the damp autumn forest, from which so much ancient folklore stems.

Other tastes also belong wholly and uniquely to Eastern Europe. They include, above all, the use of fresh dill and soured cream in salads and soups, light rye bread with caraway seeds and home-baked goods, ranging from apple strudels, poppy seed rolls to cheesecakes. By contrast, the richer soil and the long hot summers of the Balkan countries in the south mean that vegetables and fruit more often associated with the Mediterranean, such as courgettes, aubergines and peppers, melons, tomatoes, apricots and peaches, grow in abundance.

Top: This poppy seed roll is a classic example of Polish sweet yeast baking.

Left: Eastern Europe can be examined in a multitude of ways – historically, culturally, geographically, politically – and via its grand culinary traditions.

Right: Fruit picking in Skopje, Albania. Don't be surprised to find apple jam on the breakfast table down south.

Some of the more unusual recipes in this book are all-vegetable dishes from the Balkans, for example, rice and courgettes from Romania and vegetable casseroles from Serbia and Bulgaria. Rice is also prominent in Balkan dessert cookery, baked into a milk pudding and flavoured with the rose water that goes into many of their sweets.

Other local ingredients, little seen further north, include chestnuts, walnuts and sesame seeds, again used mainly in desserts.

OUTSIDE INFLUENCES

In the world of food, geographical and ethnic boundaries are often blurred. The beetroot soup variously called *borshch* and *barczsz*

is a well-known feature of Polish, Ukrainian and Russian tables, and claimed by each country as its own creation. The cooking of countries such as Hungary and Romania, combines neighbouring German and Middle Eastern elements with the use of a wide range of produce, including peppers, aubergines and brine cheeses. In Polish cooking, hints of Italian cuisine can be seen.

Ingredients have been transplanted and imported from other parts of the world, too. The many festive biscuits and honey cakes to be found in the Polish, German and Russian repertoires bear witness to the spice trade with the East, which travelled overland from China. It took the active

example of Prussian Emperor Frederick the Great in the early 18th century to encourage his people to eat the potato, newly arrived from the New World. Imported tomatoes, oranges and lemons also brought a welcome lift and colour to the local food.

THE ROLE OF RELIGION

Religion has played a part, too, in the region's cookery. In all the countries included in this book the Church has had its influence on cooking. The Orthodox tradition, in particular, imposed fasting or semi-fasting through much of the year, so there is a wide Lenten repertoire in Russian cooking. This is one of the reasons why Russian cuisine became adept at developing satisfying meat-free dishes from a restricted number of ingredients, like cabbage and beetroot. Dishes intended for days of fasting are thus the product of a highly developed culinary imagination. This is certainly true of *blini*, the Russian buckwheat pancakes, which are served with

Top: Bulgarian rice pudding, with rose water from the Valley of the Roses.

Left: Russians drinking tea made using a traditional samovar, c. 1913.

smoked fish or caviare during Carnival Week or *Maslenitsa*. The semi-fast of the week leading up to Lent, during which meat was avoided, became a celebration of other good things.

Similarly, during their long sojourn in that part of the world, Jewish cooks adapted many East European dishes to cope with the restrictions imposed by keeping a kosher kitchen, especially the injunction against eating pork. The lasting influence of Jewish cooking can be seen, for instance, in recipes for potato pancakes and carp dishes.

TYPICAL FARE
The style of cooking that begins in Germany and moves east is far removed from the gastronomic traditions of western Europe. French-style sauces, for example, are conspicuously absent. Cheese is never offered after the main course, nor is salad served as a separate digestive course. Rather, cheeses and salads of both raw and cooked vegetables, tend to appear among the copious starters that form the cold table at the start of a meal.

The ritual of the cold table is one of the great pleasures of Eastern Europe. It is here that many of their most famous dishes feature; caviare is just one example. Salted and pickled herring are also favourites, from Germany through Poland and into Russia, as are sausages. The cold table is especially well endowed with spicy, garlicky, salami-style sausages.

Despite the pressures of the working day, lunch is still the preferred big meal for families from Germany to Russia. In the Czech lands or Poland, people sit down to soup and a main course, perhaps

with a salad alongside, followed by a dessert. Further south, in Bulgaria, for example, families might enjoy tomatoes and cucumber dressed with yogurt, pork kebabs accompanied by fresh bread, with ice cream to follow.

For the main meal on special occasions, there are many fabulous recipes for beef casseroles and roasts, as well as those for chicken and goose. For everyday purposes, however, pork is the most popular meat. It is cooked in thin slices German schnitzel-style, minced into rissoles or cooked as kebabs.

Fresh cucumber salad or, even better, pickled cucumbers are a popular complement to pork. Eastern Europe is justifiably famous for its successful combination of meaty and sour flavours.

BREAD
Since bread is really at the heart of the region's good food, calling in at the baker's to buy a loaf must be one of the most satisfying food experiences of Eastern Europe. It may be white bread, made partly or

entirely with wheat, which is especially plentiful in the Ukraine. Many other areas rely more on rye than wheat to provide their staple breads. The taste and texture of these dark breads is perhaps what East Europeans miss most of all when they travel.

Yeast-leavened breads and cakes traditionally required time, loving supervision and a carefully controlled wood-fired oven. Endless hours of care were lavished on Russian *kulich* and Polish *babka* at Easter, and German *stollen* at Christmas. The peoples of Eastern Europe, whose food was tied to religious feasts and fasts as well as the vicissitudes of the harvest and the time of year, distinguished between plain and luxury food – and one way of doing this was to contrast the daily sour black bread with these grand cakes.

As more refined baking became increasingly popular in the towns, white bread made with refined flour, egg breads like the Jewish *challah* and slightly sweet buns were produced during the 19th century.

Right: Delivery of milk in Albania by traditional means.

GRAINS

Besides the grains for making bread, there are others, such as millet, barley and buckwheat (although this is not a true grain), which are used to make *kasha*. In Romania, whole areas of land are given over to maize, which is used to make cornmeal porridge, *mamaliga*, in much the same way as Italians use polenta. Millet and buckwheat are easily cooked into the nourishing porridges, soups and puddings that play an important part in a meatless or low-protein diet.

FISH

Many traditional dishes made use of fish, which were once plentiful in the waterways of the region. The rivers once teemed with fish such as tench, pike and pike-perch and from the sea came sturgeon and catfish. Environmental pollution has taken a huge toll in East Europe, while global deep-sea fishing has largely replaced locally caught river fish with deep-sea, frozen fish in the shops. Although the region's fish dishes have grown plainer and more uniform as a result, the recipes included in this book recall those earlier times.

One fish that has maintained its importance over the years, is the humble herring. Once the staple fare from Hamburg to Moscow, it is still prepared according to traditional recipes. Fresh herring is traditionally marinated with apples, pepper and oil or preserved in salt, vinegar, allspice berries and bay leaves.

SAUERKRAUT

East European cooking tends to be more sour than savoury. Pickled cabbage dishes known as sauerkraut are one successful sour example. The cabbage acquires a particular succulence and strength of flavour from the fermentation process that has made it popular right across the region, from Germany through Bohemia and Poland to Russia, and down into the Balkans.

The most delicious sauerkraut dishes include the famous *bigos*, a Polish dish, and recipes for stuffed cabbage leaves or *golubtsy*.

ALCOHOL

Alcohol is rarely used as an ingredient in East European cooking compared with the French and Italian traditions. In many regions where climate and soil would have supported wine making, it never really flowered in the past, and this is partly due to religious influences. Muslim-dominated south-east Europe certainly did not cook with wine, and these countries have only relatively recently started to produce and export it. Catholic and Protestant lands were more tolerant, and for centuries flowery white wines have been produced and drunk in western and southern Germany, south Bohemia and Moravia. Today, a wide range of

Top: Polish bigos *was originally cooked in the forest for aristocratic hunting parties because it could be succesfully reheated over an open fire.*

Left: Baking bread in a wood oven according to traditional peasant methods.

new global market-quality table wines have built on old traditions in Hungary and Romania and encouraged new ones in Bulgaria, Serbia and Montenegro. Even so, these are not wine-drinking cultures such as the Mediterranean.

In Central and Eastern Europe lager beer or spirits such as vodka, brewed from rye or potatoes, are generally the preferred drinks to accompany a meal. The vodka is high quality, as are the excellent fruit brandies characteristic of the southern countries.

HOME COOKING
Until very recently, food right across Eastern Europe was best bought in local markets, where the sauerkraut was weighed out from

wooden barrels and the paprika was spooned into newspaper cornets. Live chickens, honey, slabs of curd and brine cheese would all be on offer, alongside stalls selling fruit, vegetables and herbs. The baker would also not be far away from the marketplace.

As none of the East European cuisines has been restaurant-led, the lucky traveller in Eastern Europe could be invited into a private house to sample local dishes. Whatever the food offered, the guest is always likely to receive a splendid gastronomic welcome.

For the reader at home, this book provides a comprehensive collection of recipes that reflect pride in the traditional tables of each locality. Grouped according to

region, typical dishes suited to both ordinary and elaborate occasions are on offer. They can be enjoyed and sampled by any cook anywhere in the world.

Largely due to the region's 50 years of political isolation from market influences, the East European way of eating has gone more or less untouched by modern views of what constitutes a healthy diet. However, the recipes in this book have been lightened and reduced in calories, to suit present-day Western preferences and nutritional concerns.

East European cooking is often economical because it mainly encapsulates peasant culinary traditions. It requires not fancy ingredients, but rather a willingness to put in some time in the kitchen – something that is well worth doing in order to create these recipes and reproduce the tastes and textures of really good food.

Top: The much-loved Black Forest Cherry Cake is truly delicious and comes from southern Germany where Kirsch is distilled.

Left: Open-air cafe in Vienna, watercolour by Wilhelm Gause, 1901.

RUSSIA, POLAND AND THE UKRAINE

The cooking of this area forms one of the classic cuisines of the world, encapsulating all the characteristics of traditional cooking that has remained virtually unchanged for centuries. Be it a humble beetroot soup or the glories of caviare, the ingredients, flavours and textures all show how good cooking really should be.

INTRODUCTION

The region occupied by Russia, Poland and the Ukraine has a tradition of peasant cooking, defined by the tart flavours of sourdough rye bread, pickles and sauerkraut, and complemented by mushrooms, herring, onion and sausage. These simple foods reflect what the often poor soil yielded in the harsh climate, and what could be preserved by traditional means (in salt or vinegar or by drying) for year-round use. Hardy root and vegetable crops, a variety of grains, the flavours of garlic, mustard and horseradish, and sour dairy products, such as yogurt and buttermilk (the Russian *kefir),* were the region's staples. Cabbage and cucumbers, fresh or pickled, were the primary sources of vitamin C in what, for centuries, was a highly restricted diet.

RELIGIOUS INFLUENCES

In Russia and those parts of the Ukraine where the Russian Orthodox Church determined popular eating habits, at least until the beginning of the 20th century, the Church made a virtue out of economic necessity. It divided foods into two groups. For over half the days of the year only Lenten fare was allowed: vegetables, fish and mushrooms. Milk, eggs and meat were permitted on the remaining days.

The result of this intervention was a good number of simple, versatile recipes. A full meal might consist of a cabbage soup with a grain porridge called *kasha*. Meat, if available, would be cooked in the soup but served separately afterwards. On full fast days, mushrooms could be substituted for meat to give the soup flavour and perhaps to fill little pies or *pirozhki* to eat alongside it.

Buckwheat pancakes and soured cream, typical of the meat-free Carnival Week, now rank among the best-liked Russian dishes in the world. Russian Easter food, centred on roast suckling pig basted in soured cream and a cake, *kulich,* served with a sweet cream cheese, is a splendidly rich contrast with the simpler Lenten food that precedes it.

In Poland, there are 12 Lenten dishes – to equal the number of apostles – including a beetroot soup, herring, carp in black sauce and a mushroom dish. Christmas is an important time for the Roman Catholic Church and the elaborate Polish meal on Christmas Eve is gastronomically typical.

RECENT CHANGES

Two factors in the 19th century began to modernize the East European peasant diet. One was the industrialization that brought peasants into the towns and saw middle-class cooking influenced by cosmopolitan ideas. The other was the impact of the eating habits of the royal courts on the cuisines of both Russia and Poland, which eventually filtered down through the aristocracy to the bourgeoisie.

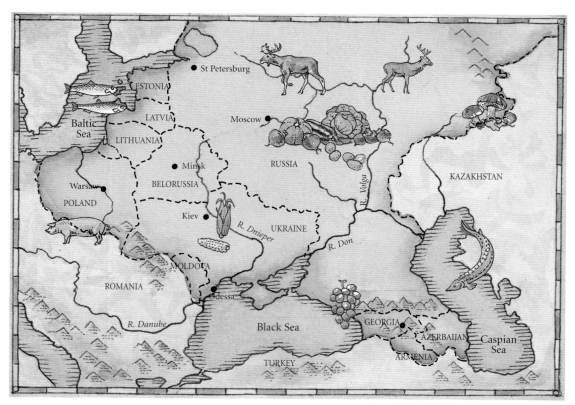

Left: The recipes in this section cover an area that stretches from the Baltic Sea in the north to the Caspian and Black Seas in the south. From Russia, the Baltic countries and Poland in the north, through the Ukraine and down to the edge of Turkey and the Middle East, these recipes reflect the wonderful diversity and the overall defining culinary characteristics of classic East European food.

Right: Open-air cooking on a large scale in Yakut, former USSR.

THE ROYAL COURTS

The Polish court flourished in the 16th century, when Poland's empire stretched from the Baltic to the Black Sea and the educated minority enjoyed an artistic and political culture, rich in contacts with Renaissance Europe. The Italian connection was particularly strong, due to the Italian-born Queen Bona Sforza who brought with her an entourage and ideas about cooking when she married King Sigismund in 1518. As a consequence, southern European vegetables were planted in the garden of the Royal Court at Krakow. Bona Sforza is also associated with Polish ice cream, pasta and cakes – Polish *babka* being really a first cousin to Italian *panettone*.

In the 19th century, access to French cookery books led to Polish cooking becoming richer than Russian in, for example, sauces and composite tastes. At the same time, however, the Russian upper classes also felt under constant pressure to "Frenchify" their own cooking, the court and aristocracy mainly employing French chefs to produce elaborate dishes, replete with butter and cream. Antonïn Carême, as cook to Alexander I (Tsar 1801–25), began a task that was continued by four generations of foreign chefs up to the Russian Revolution.

Generally, however, there was always opposition to this outside influence, and patriotic palates preferred the traditional breads, grains and soups. One such example is *borshch*, the famous beetroot soup, whose origin cannot be fixed within any present-day national confines. It can be served as a consommé or as a thick soup.

By contrast the Russian cold table, originally borrowed from Scandinavia during the reign of the

great Westernizing tsar, Peter I (Tsar 1682-1725), has been wholly incorporated into the national cuisine as the classic first course. Comprising little open sandwich

hors d'oeuvres, these *zakuski* dishes, which are washed down with ice-cold vodka, deserve their fame, especially as the jewel of the *zakuski* table is often caviare.

INGREDIENTS

VEGETABLES AND MUSHROOMS

Ridge cucumbers, with a firm texture and full flavour, are either used fresh in salads or pickled in bottles for winter. Other popular vegetables are beetroot, potato, carrots, parsnips and fresh cabbage, all of which grow well in a cold climate and can be stored all year round. Cabbage is also fermented in brine, with spices, to make the widely available sauerkraut. As for spring onions, both the white bulbs and the green tips contribute to the characteristic flavour of East European composite salads.

The romance of mushroom hunting belongs to the forests of Eastern Europe, where many varieties are found. Mushrooms are dried for use in soups and sauces, or salted or pickled for snacks with bread and vodka. They are also sautéed fresh in butter and herbs, or sauced with soured cream.

Top left, clockwise from left: pickled beetroot, sauerkraut, pickled cucumbers, dill pickles and caperberries.

Top right, clockwise: red and white cabbage, beetroot, cucumbers, mushrooms, parsnips, potatoes and carrots.

Right, from top left: Black and red lumpfish roe, salmon caviar, pike, salmon, carp and herring.

FISH

The most celebrated fish of this region belong to the sturgeon family. Of this family, both the beluga and the sevruga produce the highly prized black caviare. Freshwater salmon varieties are also very important, both for their firm flesh and for the "red" caviare so often seen on *zakuski* tables. Carp is traditional in Poland and is nowadays farmed. Herring is popular everywhere, although increasingly only the canned product is available. Pike, perch and pike-perch are the grand old river fish, yielding a firm white flesh that is suitable for pies and baked fish dishes.

DAIRY PRODUCTS

Soured cream takes the place of an oil in dressing East European salads of raw and cooked vegetables. It is the essential accompaniment to soups and pancakes and the basis for modern sauced dishes such as Beef Stroganov. It is also used in baking cakes and biscuits.

The traditional East European cheeses are made with cow's milk and are young and mild. Curd cheese is used to make savoury dips and *paskha*, the sweet Easter cream. Curd cheese can be used alone or with other ingredients to make savoury or sweet patties; it is also used to stuff pasta and pies, and forms the basis for the traditional cheesecake. *Brinza*, similar to Greek feta, is a brine cheese common all over Eastern and Central Europe, which appears in starters and pies.

MEAT DISHES

Sucking pig is a traditional Russian delicacy, as is the game bird called *ryabchik*, or hazel-hen. Plentiful use is made of beef for braising and stewing. Polish sausage is made of top-quality pork and veal, flavoured with garlic and mustard seed.

GRAINS

The Russian word *kasha* and the related words in Polish and Ukrainian denote any cooked grain. Semolina, millet, oats and buckwheat are eaten at breakfast, usually cooked in water or milk and served with butter. Buckwheat, rice, millet or barley accompany savoury dishes. Buckwheat, actually a relative of the rhubarb family rather than a grain, is cooked into *kasha* and its flour is used to make traditional Shrovetide pancakes, or *blini*. It grows prolifically in Eastern Europe, and its recognizable smoky taste is characteristic of traditional peasant cooking.

Sourdough breads from this area have a distinctive, satisfying quality, thanks to their being made with rye flour by a sour fermentation process. This produces long-lasting loaves with excellent digestive properties, ranging from straw-coloured bread to the distinctly black Russian *borodinsky*, which is made with molasses and has its crust studded with coriander seeds.

HERBS, SPICES AND OTHER FLAVOURINGS

Dill, the most common herb in Eastern and Central European cooking, adds a distinct freshness to pickles as well as to salads and cooked dishes. The feathery leaves needed for authentic cooking lose much of their taste when dried so they should always be used fresh. The pungent seeds can be used in sauerkraut dishes and stews. Parsley, of the pungent, flat leaf variety, is also widely used in soups and salads and as a garnish, while the root adds flavour to stocks and soup bases. Fresh garlic adds piquancy to soups and stews, while mustard and horseradish give bite to fish and meat dishes.

FRUIT

East Europe has a strong tradition of domestic jam-making and bottling every available fruit and vegetable, from excellent plum jam to pickled spiced tomatoes. Less solid jams, which preserve the whole fruits, such as Russian

blackcurrant *varen'ye*, are traditionally served in a small saucer with tea, or to accompany a breakfast bowl of semolina *kasha*.

DRINKS

Russians drink tea that is either imported from the Far East or grown in Georgia. The tea is brewed in a small pot on top of the samovar, and diluted with water from the urn below. In Poland, under strong Central European and Italian influence, coffee is more popular. As for alcohol, both Poland and Russia claim to be the home of vodka, which has been made in Eastern Europe since at least the 15th century. Distilled, ideally from rye, it is then purified and water added. Small additions of barley, oats, buckwheat or wheat, herbs and tree bark give further flavour. Additions to the finished vodka make for specialities such as pepper vodka, which is used as a remedy for colds. Plain vodka is best for the *zakuski* table, however, served ice cold and downed in a single gulp.

Top, clockwise from back: dill, flat-leaved parsley, sour cream, cream, horseradish and fresh garlic bulbs.

Left, clockwise from top left: buckwheat flour, semolina, whole rolled porridge oats, pot barley, millet and raw buckwheat (centre).

SOUPS AND STARTERS

The classic soups of Eastern Europe have remained unchanged for centuries. Shchi, based on cabbage, is a north Russian speciality, while borshch is made from beetroot and is popular in the south and throughout Poland and the Ukraine. The balance of sweet and sour is typical, with the use of fermented juice or pickled vegetables. Many hors d'oeuvres served in the west originated as Russian starters. Caviare is probably the most famous of these, traditionally served with small glasses of ice-cold vodka.

Pea and Barley Soup

This thick and warming soup, *Grochowka*, makes a substantial starter, or it may be served as a meal in its own right, eaten with hot crusty bread.

INGREDIENTS

Serves 6
225g/8oz/1¼ cups yellow split peas
25g/1oz/¼ cup pearl barley
1.75 litres/3 pints/7½ cups vegetable
  or ham stock
50g/2oz smoked streaky bacon, cubed
25g/1oz/2 tbsp butter
1 onion, finely chopped
2 garlic cloves, crushed
225g/8oz celeriac, cubed
15ml/1 tbsp chopped fresh marjoram
salt and freshly ground black pepper
bread, to serve

1 Rinse the peas and barley in a sieve under cold running water. Put in a bowl, cover with plenty of water and leave to soak overnight.

2 The next day, drain and rinse the peas and barley. Put them in a large pan, pour in the stock and bring to the boil. Turn down the heat and simmer gently for 40 minutes.

3 Dry fry the bacon cubes in a frying pan for 5 minutes, or until well browned and crispy. Remove with a slotted spoon, leaving the fat behind, and set aside.

4 Add the butter to the frying pan, add the onion and garlic and cook gently for 5 minutes. Add the celeriac and cook for a further 5 minutes, or until the onion is just starting to colour.

5 Add the softened vegetables and bacon to the pan of stock, peas and barley. Season lightly with salt and pepper, then cover and simmer for 20 minutes, or until the soup is thick. Stir in the marjoram, add extra black pepper to taste and serve with bread.

Borshch

Beetroot is the main ingredient of *Borshch*, and its flavour and colour dominate this well-known soup. It is a classic of both Russia and Poland.

INGREDIENTS

Serves 4–6

900g/2lb uncooked beetroot, peeled
2 carrots, peeled
2 celery sticks
40g/1½ oz/3 tbsp butter
2 onions, sliced
2 garlic cloves, crushed
4 tomatoes, peeled, seeded and chopped
1 bay leaf
1 large parsley sprig
2 cloves
4 whole peppercorns
1.2 litres/2 pints/5 cups beef or chicken stock
150ml/¼ pint/⅔ cup beetroot *kvas* (see *Cook's Tip*) or the liquid from pickled beetroot
salt and freshly ground black pepper
soured cream, garnished with snipped fresh chives or sprigs of dill, to serve

1 Cut the beetroot, carrots and celery into fairly thick strips. Melt the butter in a large pan and cook the onions over a low heat for 5 minutes, stirring occasionally.

2 Add the beetroot, carrots and celery and cook for a further 5 minutes, stirring occasionally.

3 Add the garlic and chopped tomatoes to the pan and cook, stirring, for 2 more minutes.

4 Place the bay leaf, parsley, cloves and peppercorns in a piece of muslin and tie with string.

5 Add the muslin bag to the pan with the stock. Bring to the boil, reduce the heat, cover and simmer for 1¼ hours, or until the vegetables are very tender. Discard the bag. Stir in the beetroot *kvas* and season. Bring to the boil. Ladle into bowls and serve with soured cream garnished with chives or dill.

COOK'S TIP

Beetroot *kvas*, fermented beetroot juice, adds an intense colour and a slight tartness. If unavailable, peel and grate 1 beetroot, add 150ml/¼ pint/⅔ cup stock and 10ml/2 tsp lemon juice. Bring to the boil, cover and leave for 30 minutes. Strain before using.

Fresh Cabbage Shchi

This version of Russia's national dish is made from fresh cabbage rather than sauerkraut.

INGREDIENTS

Serves 4–6
1 small turnip
2 carrots
40g/1½ oz/3 tbsp butter
1 large onion, sliced
2 celery sticks, sliced
1 white cabbage, about 675g/1½ lb
1.2 litres/2 pints/5 cups beef stock
1 sharp eating apple, cored, peeled
   and chopped
2 bay leaves
5ml/1 tsp chopped fresh dill
10ml/2 tsp pickled cucumber juice
   or lemon juice
salt and freshly ground black pepper
fresh herbs, to garnish
soured cream and black bread, to serve

1 Cut the turnip and carrots into matchstick strips. Melt the butter in a large pan and fry the turnip, carrot, onion and celery for 10 minutes.

2 Shred the cabbage, and add to the pan with the stock, apple, bay leaves and dill and bring to the boil. Cover and simmer for 40 minutes or until the vegetables are really tender.

3 Remove the bay leaves, then stir in the pickled cucumber juice or lemon juice and season with plenty of salt and pepper. Serve hot, garnished with fresh herbs and accompanied by soured cream and black bread.

Sorrel and Spinach Soup

This is an excellent Russian summer soup. If sorrel is unavailable, use double the amount of spinach instead and add a dash of lemon juice to the soup just before serving.

INGREDIENTS

Serves 4
25g/1oz/2 tbsp butter
225g/8oz sorrel, washed and
   stalks removed
225g/8oz young spinach, washed and
   stalks removed
25g/1oz fresh horseradish, grated
750ml/1¼ pints/3 cups *kvas* or cider
1 pickled cucumber, finely chopped
30ml/2 tbsp chopped fresh dill
225g/8oz cooked fish, such as pike,
   perch or salmon, skinned and boned
salt and freshly ground black pepper
sprig of dill, to garnish

1 Melt the butter in a large pan. Add the sorrel and spinach leaves and fresh horseradish. Cover and gently cook for 3–4 minutes, or until the leaves are wilted.

COOK'S TIP

Kvas is a Russian beer made by fermenting wheat, rye and buckwheat.

---

2 Spoon into a food processor and process to a fine purée. Ladle into a tureen or bowl and stir in the *kvas* or cider, cucumber and dill.

3 Chop the fish into bite-size pieces. Add to the soup, then season with plenty of salt and pepper. Chill for at least 3 hours before serving, garnished with a sprig of dill.

Mixed Mushroom Solyanka

The tart flavours of pickled cucumber, capers and lemon adds extra bite to this rich soup.

INGREDIENTS

Serves 4

2 onions, chopped
1.2 litres/2 pints/5 cups vegetable
  stock
450g/1lb/6 cups mushrooms, sliced
20ml/4 tsp tomato purée
1 pickled cucumber, chopped
1 bay leaf
15ml/1 tbsp capers in brine, drained
pinch of salt
6 peppercorns, crushed
lemon rind curls, green olives and
  sprigs of flat leaf parsley, to garnish

1 Put the onions in a large pan with 50ml/2fl oz/¼ cup of the stock. Cook, stirring occasionally, until the liquid has evaporated.

2 Add the remaining vegetable stock with the sliced mushrooms, bring to the boil, cover and simmer gently for 30 minutes.

3 In a small bowl, blend the tomato purée with 30ml/2 tbsp of stock.

4 Add the tomato purée to the pan with the pickled cucumber, bay leaf, capers, salt and peppercorns. Cook gently for 10 more minutes.

5 Ladle the soup into warmed bowls and sprinkle lemon rind curls, a few olives and a sprig of flat leaf parley over each bowl before serving.

Grandfather's Soup

This soup derives its name from the fact that it is easily digested and therefore thought to be suitable for the elderly.

INGREDIENTS

Serves 4
1 large onion, finely sliced
25g/1oz/2 tbsp butter
350g/12oz potatoes, peeled and diced
900ml/1½ pints/3¾ cups beef stock
1 bay leaf
salt and freshly ground black pepper

For the drop noodles
75g/3oz/⅔ cup self-raising flour
pinch of salt
15g/½oz/1 tbsp butter
15ml/1 tbsp chopped fresh parsley,
    plus a little extra to garnish
1 egg, beaten
chunks of bread, to serve

1 In a wide heavy-based pan, cook the onion in the butter gently for 10 minutes, or until it begins to brown.

2 Add the diced potatoes and cook for 2–3 minutes, then pour in the stock. Add the bay leaf, salt and pepper. Bring to the boil, then reduce the heat, cover and simmer for 10 minutes.

COOK'S TIP

Use old potatoes, of a floury texture, such as King Edward or Maris Piper.

3 Meanwhile, make the noodles. Sift the flour and salt into a bowl and rub in the butter. Stir in the parsley, then add the egg to the flour mixture and mix to a soft dough.

4 Drop half-teaspoonfuls of the dough into the simmering soup. Cover and simmer gently for a further 10 minutes. Ladle the soup into warmed soup bowls, scatter over a little parsley, and serve immediately with chunks of bread.

Eggs with Caviare

Caviare is the roe from the huge sturgeon fish that swim in the Caspian Sea. It is often served on its own, in a bowl set over crushed ice, with a glass of chilled neat vodka. Alternatively, it may be used sparingly, as in this Ukrainian recipe, as a garnish.

INGREDIENTS

Serves 4
6 eggs, hard-boiled and halved, lengthways
4 spring onions, very finely sliced
30ml/2 tbsp mayonnaise
1.5ml/¼ tsp Dijon mustard
25g/1oz/2 tbsp caviare or black lumpfish roe
salt and freshly ground black pepper
small sprigs of dill, to garnish
watercress, to serve

1 Remove the yolks from the halved eggs. Mash the yolks to a smooth paste in a bowl with the spring onions, mayonnaise and mustard. Mix well and season with salt and pepper.

2 Fill the egg whites with the yolk mixture and arrange them on a serving dish. Spoon a little caviare or roe on top of each before serving with watercress.

——————— TYPES OF CAVIARE ———————

Beluga is the largest member of the sturgeon family, and the eggs are a pearly-grey colour. **Oscietra** comes from a smaller sturgeon, and the eggs have a golden tinge. **Sevruga** caviare is less expensive than other types, as it produces eggs at a much younger age. **Lumpfish roe,** not a true caviare, has black or orange eggs. **Salmon roe**, from the red salmon, has large, translucent pinky-orange eggs.

Aubergine "Caviare"

The word "caviare" is used to describe spreads and dips made from cooked vegetables. The aubergine is the vegetable most widely used in this way, and many Ukrainian families have their own secret recipe.

INGREDIENTS

Serves 4–6
1.5kg/3lb aubergines
1 onion, very finely chopped
1 garlic clove, crushed
75ml/5 tbsp olive oil
450g/1lb tomatoes, peeled and chopped
5ml/1 tsp lemon juice
150ml/¼ pint/⅔ cup natural yogurt
5ml/1 tsp salt
freshly ground black pepper
spring onion slices, to garnish
toasted bread twists, to serve

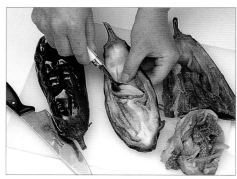

1 Preheat the oven to 180°C/350°F/ Gas 4. Put the aubergines on an oiled rack over a roasting tin. Bake in the oven for 25–30 minutes, or until soft. Leave to cool.

2 Meanwhile, fry the finely chopped onion and garlic in 15ml/1 tbsp of the oil for 10 minutes.

3 Using a spoon, remove the baked aubergine flesh, then purée in a food processor until smooth. With the motor running, add the remaining oil.

4 Spoon into a bowl. Stir in the onions, tomatoes, lemon juice and yogurt, salt and pepper to taste. Cover with clear film and chill for 4 hours. To serve, garnish with spring onions and accompany with toasted bread twists.

Herring Pâté

Vast quantities of herring are fished in the Baltic Sea to the north of Poland. A traditional Polish hors d'oeuvre, *Pasta Śledziowa* is usually served with tiny glasses of ice-cold vodka.

INGREDIENTS

Serves 4
2 fresh herrings, filleted
50g/2oz/4 tbsp butter, softened
5ml/1 tsp creamed horseradish sauce
freshly ground black pepper

To serve
4 slices rye bread
1 small onion, cut into rings
1 red eating apple, cored and sliced
15ml/1 tbsp lemon juice
45ml/3 tbsp soured cream

1 Chop the herrings into pieces and put in a food processor with the butter, horseradish sauce and pepper. Process until smooth.

2 Spoon the herring pâté into a bowl. Cover with clear film and chill for at least 1 hour.

3 Serve the pâté on rye bread, add onion rings and apple slices, tossed in lemon juice. Top with a little soured cream and garnish with dill.

Little Finger Biscuits

These savoury Polish biscuits, *paluszki*, are delicious served warm or cold with soup or dips, or on their own as a snack.

INGREDIENTS

Makes 30
115g/4oz/8 tbsp butter, softened
115g/4oz/1⅓ cups mashed potato
150g/5oz/1¼ cups plain flour, plus
  extra for dusting
2.5ml/½ tsp salt
1 egg, beaten
30ml/2 tbsp caraway seeds

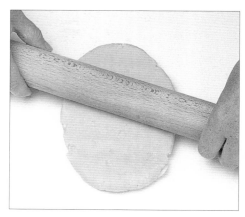

1 Preheat the oven to 220°C/425°F/ Gas 7. Put the butter and mashed potato in a large bowl. Sift the flour and salt into the bowl, then mix to a soft dough.

2 Knead the dough on a lightly floured surface for a few seconds, or until smooth. Wrap in clear film and chill for 30 minutes.

3 Roll out the potato dough on a lightly floured surface until 8mm/⅓in thick. Brush with beaten egg, then cut into strips 2 × 7.5cm/ ¾ × 3in. Transfer to an oiled baking sheet and sprinkle with caraway seeds.

4 Bake for 12 minutes, or until lightly browned. Transfer to a wire rack and leave to cool. Store in an airtight container.

Pirozhki

Homemade *pirozhki* are great favourites of old and young alike. They look splendid piled high and golden brown.

INGREDIENTS

Makes 35
225g/8oz/2 cups strong white flour
2.5ml/½ tsp salt
2.5ml/½ tsp caster sugar
5ml/1 tsp easy-blend dried yeast
25g/1oz/2 tbsp butter, softened
1 egg, beaten, plus a little extra
90ml/6 tbsp warm milk

For the filling
1 small onion, finely chopped
175g/6oz minced chicken
15ml/1 tbsp sunflower oil
75ml/5 tbsp chicken stock
30ml/2 tbsp chopped fresh parsley
pinch of grated nutmeg
salt and freshly ground black pepper

1 Sift the flour, salt and sugar into a large bowl. Stir in the dried yeast, then make a well in the centre.

2 Add the butter, egg and milk and mix to a soft dough. Turn on to a lightly floured surface and knead for 10 minutes, until smooth and elastic.

3 Put the dough in a clean bowl, cover with clear film and leave in a warm place to rise for 1 hour, or until the dough has doubled in size.

4 Meanwhile, fry the onion and chicken in the oil for 10 minutes. Add the stock and simmer for 5 minutes. Stir in the parsley, nutmeg and salt and pepper. Leave to cool.

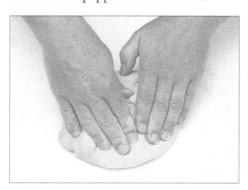

5 Preheat the oven to 220°C/425°F/ Gas 7. Knead the dough, then roll out until 3mm/⅛in thick. Stamp out rounds with a 7.5cm/3in cutter.

6 Brush the edges with beaten egg. Put a little filling in the middle, then press the edges together. Leave to rise on oiled baking sheets, covered with oiled clear film, for 15 minutes. Brush with a little more egg. Bake for 5 minutes, then for 10 minutes at 190°C/375°F/ Gas 5, until well risen.

Buckwheat Blini

Traditionally eaten during the
meatless week before Lent, both
sweet and savoury toppings can
be used; soured cream and
caviare is the most famous.

INGREDIENTS

Serves 4
75g/3oz/²/₃ cup plain flour
50g/2oz/¹/₂ cup buckwheat or
    wheatmeal flour
2.5ml/¹/₂ tsp salt
5ml/1 tsp easy-blend dried yeast
175ml/6fl oz/³/₄ cup warm milk
25g/1oz/2 tbsp butter, melted
1 egg, separated
45ml/3 tbsp oil

For the toppings
150ml/5fl oz/²/₃ cup soured cream
30ml/2 tbsp chopped fresh dill
50g/2oz/4 tbsp red or black
    lumpfish roe
115g/4oz smoked mackerel, skinned,
    boned and flaked
50g/2oz/4 tbsp unsalted butter,
    softened
finely grated rind of ¹/₂ lemon
shredded lemon rind, to garnish
lemon wedges, to serve

1 Sift the flours and salt into a large
bowl, adding any bran left in the
sieve. Stir in the easy-blend yeast, then
make a well in the centre.

2 Pour in the milk and gradually beat
in the flour until smooth. Cover
with clear film and leave to rise for
1 hour, or until doubled in size.

3 Stir in the melted butter and egg
yolk. Whisk the egg white in a
bowl until stiff and then gently fold in.
Cover and leave to stand for 20 minutes.

4 Heat 15ml/1 tbsp of the oil in a
large, heavy frying pan over a
medium heat and drop in about
4 spoonfuls of batter. Cook for 1–2
minutes, or until bubbles appear on top.

5 Turn them over and cook for a
further 1 minute, or until both
sides are brown. Remove the *blini* from
the pan and keep them moist in a
folded clean dish towel.

6 Repeat the process with the
remaining batter, adding a little oil
to the pan when needed, to make
about 24 *blini*. Allow to cool.

7 Arrange the *blini* on a serving plate.
Use the soured cream and chopped
dill to top half of the *blini*. Spoon 5ml/
1 tsp lumpfish roe on top of the soured
cream and dill.

8 In another bowl, mix the smoked
mackerel, butter and lemon rind
together and use to top the remaining
blini. Garnish with shredded lemon
rind. Serve with lemon wedges.

Olivier Salad

In the 1880s the French chef, Olivier, opened a restaurant in Moscow called the Hermitage. It became one of the most famous dining clubs in the city, where many innovative dishes were served. Olivier later published a book of everyday Russian cooking and gave his name to this elaborate salad.

INGREDIENTS

Serves 6

2 young grouse or partridges
6 juniper berries, crushed
40g/1½oz/3 tbsp butter, softened
2 small onions, each stuck with
   3 cloves
2 streaky bacon rashers, halved
10 baby potatoes, unpeeled
1 cucumber
2 Little Gem lettuces, separated
   into leaves
2 eggs, hard-boiled and quartered

For the dressing

1 egg yolk
5ml/1 tsp Dijon mustard
175ml/6fl oz/¾ cup light olive oil
60ml/4 tbsp white wine vinegar
salt and freshly ground black pepper

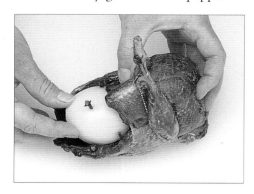

1 Preheat the oven to 200°C/400°F/
Gas 6. Put the grouse or partridges in a small roasting tin. Mix the juniper berries and the butter together and tuck half the juniper butter and one clove-studded onion into the vent of each of the birds.

2 Lay 2 bacon pieces over each breast. Roast for 30 minutes, or until the juices run only slightly pink when the thigh is pierced with a skewer.

3 Leave to cool, then cut the meat into 2.5cm/1in pieces.

4 Meanwhile, cook the potatoes in boiling salted water for about 20 minutes, or until tender. Allow to cool, then peel and cut into 1cm/½in slices.

COOK'S TIP

Cold roast beef can be used instead of the game, if you prefer.

5 Cut a few slices of cucumber for garnishing and set aside. Halve the remaining cucumber lengthways, remove the seeds and dice.

6 To make the dressing, put the egg yolk, mustard and a little salt and pepper in a small bowl and whisk together. Add the olive oil in a thin stream, whisking all the time until thickened, then stir in the vinegar.

7 Put the pieces of meat, potato and cucumber in a bowl. Pour over half the dressing and mix carefully. Arrange the lettuce leaves on a serving platter and pile the salad in the middle.

8 Garnish with the reserved cucumber slices and the quartered hard-boiled eggs. Serve with the remaining dressing.

MEAT AND POULTRY

Although beef, poultry and game are eaten in Russia, Poland and the Ukraine, pork is by far the most popular meat. Whole joints are usually marinated to produce tender and succulent meat, and pork is the main ingredient of kielbasa, *the famous Polish sausage exported all over the world. Throughout the region, frequent food shortages in history have called for ingenuity in making a little go a long way, and many recipes reflect this by cleverly combining a number of meats with herbs, spices and pickled vegetables.*

Liver and Bacon Varenyky

There is an old Ukrainian superstition that if *varenyky* are counted, the dough will split and the filling spill out.

INGREDIENTS

Serves 4
200g/7oz/1¾ cups plain flour
1.5ml/¼ tsp salt
2 eggs, beaten
15g/½oz/1 tbsp butter, melted
beaten egg, for sealing
15ml/1 tbsp sunflower oil

For the filling
15ml/1 tbsp sunflower oil
½ small onion, finely chopped
115g/4oz smoked streaky bacon, roughly chopped
225g/8oz chicken or lamb's liver, roughly chopped
30ml/2 tbsp snipped fresh chives, plus extra for garnish
salt and freshly ground black pepper

1 Sift the flour and salt into a bowl. Make a well in the centre. Add the eggs and butter and mix to a dough.

2 Knead the dough on a lightly floured surface for 2–3 minutes, until smooth. Wrap in clear film and leave to rest for 30 minutes.

3 For the filling, heat the oil in a pan and cook the onion for 5 minutes. Add the bacon and cook for a further 4–5 minutes. Stir in the liver and cook for 1 minute, until browned.

4 Put the liver mixture in a food processor or blender and process until it is finely chopped, but not smooth. Add the snipped chives and season with salt and pepper. Process for a few more seconds.

5 Roll out the dough on a lightly floured surface until 3mm/⅛in thick. Stamp out rounds of dough with a 5cm/2in cutter.

6 Spoon a teaspoon of filling into the middle of each round. Brush the edges of the dough with beaten egg and fold in half to make half-moon shapes. Leave to dry on a floured dish towel for 30 minutes.

7 Bring a pan of salted water to the boil. Add the oil, then add the *varenyky*, in batches if necessary. Bring back to the boil and cook them at a gentle simmer for 10 minutes, until tender. Drain well and serve hot, garnished with snipped chives. Serve with fresh capers.

Roast Loin of Pork with Apple Stuffing

A spit-roasted sucking pig, basted with butter or cream and served with an apple in its mouth, was a classic dish for the Russian festive table. This roasted loin with crisp crackling makes a less expensive alternative.

INGREDIENTS

Serves 6–8

1.75kg/4lb boned loin of pork
300ml/½ pint/1¼ cups dry cider
150ml/¼ pint/⅔ cup soured cream
7.5ml/1½ tsp sea salt

For the stuffing

25g/1oz/2 tbsp butter
1 small onion, chopped
50g/2oz/1 cup fresh white
 breadcrumbs
2 apples, cored, peeled and chopped
50g/2oz/scant ½ cup raisins
finely grated rind of 1 orange
pinch of ground cloves
salt and freshly ground black pepper

1 Preheat the oven to 220°C/425°F/ Gas 7. To make the stuffing, melt the butter in a pan and gently fry the onion for 10 minutes, or until soft. Stir into the remaining stuffing ingredients.

2 Put the pork, rind side down, on a board. Make a horizontal cut between the meat and outer layer of fat, cutting to within 2.5cm/1in of the edges to make a pocket.

3 Push the stuffing into the pocket. Roll up lengthways and tie with string. Score the rind at 2cm/¾in intervals with a sharp knife.

COOK'S TIP

Do not baste during the final 2 hours of roasting, so that the crackling becomes crisp.

4 Pour the cider and soured cream into a casserole, in which the joint just fits. Stir to combine, then add the pork, rind side down. Cook, uncovered, in the oven for 30 minutes.

5 Turn the joint over, so that the rind is on top. Baste with the juices, then sprinkle the rind with sea salt. Cook for 1 hour, basting after 30 minutes.

6 Reduce the oven temperature to 180°C/350°F/Gas 4. Cook for a further 1½ hours. Leave the joint to stand for 20 minutes before carving.

Russian Hamburgers

Every Russian family has its own version of this homely hamburger. The mixture can also be shaped into small round meatballs known as *bitki*, which make irresistible snacks.

INGREDIENTS

Serves 4
115g/4oz/2 cups fresh white
  breadcrumbs
45ml/3 tbsp milk
450g/1lb finely minced beef, lamb
  or veal
1 egg, beaten
30ml/2 tbsp plain flour
30ml/2 tbsp sunflower oil
salt and freshly ground black pepper
tomato sauce, pickled vegetables and
  crispy fried onions, to serve

1 Put the breadcrumbs in a bowl and spoon over the milk. Leave to soak for 10 minutes. Add the minced meat, egg, salt and pepper and mix all the ingredients together thoroughly.

2 Divide the mixture into 4 equal portions and shape into ovals, each about 10cm/4in long and 5cm/2in wide. Coat each with the flour.

3 Heat the oil in a frying pan and fry the burgers for about 8 minutes on each side. Serve with a tomato sauce, pickled vegetables and fried onions.

Beef Stroganov

At the end of the 19th century, Alexander Stroganov gave his name to this now well-known Russian dish of beef and onions cooked with cream, and it became his signature dish when entertaining at his home in Odessa. Finely cut potato chips are the classic accompaniment.

INGREDIENTS

Serves 4
450g/1lb fillet or rump steak, trimmed
15ml/1 tbsp sunflower oil
25g/1oz/2 tbsp unsalted butter
1 onion, sliced
15ml/1 tbsp plain flour
5ml/1 tsp tomato purée
5ml/1 tsp Dijon mustard
5ml/1 tsp lemon juice
150ml/¼ pint/⅔ cup soured cream
salt and freshly ground black pepper
fresh herbs, to garnish

1 Place the steak between 2 oiled sheets of clear film. Gently beat with a rolling pin to flatten and tenderize the meat. Cut it into thin strips about 5cm/2in long.

2 Heat the remaining oil and half the butter in a frying pan and fry the beef over a high heat for 2 minutes, or until browned. Remove the strips of beef from the pan with a slotted spoon, leaving any juices behind.

3 Melt the remaining butter in the pan and gently fry the onion for 10 minutes, until soft.

4 Sprinkle over the flour then stir it in, followed by the tomato purée, mustard, lemon juice and soured cream. Return the beef to the pan and stir until the sauce is bubbling. Season to taste with salt and pepper, and then serve immediately, garnished with fresh herbs, with deep-fried potato chips.

Bigos

Poland's national dish, *bigos*, is best made a day in advance.

INGREDIENTS

Serves 8

15g/½oz/¼ cup dried mushrooms
225g/8oz/1 cup stoned prunes
225g/8oz lean boneless pork
225g/8oz lean boneless venison
225g/8oz chuck steak
225g/8oz *kielbasa* (see Cook's Tip)
25g/1oz/¼ cup plain flour
2 onions, sliced
45ml/3 tbsp olive oil
60ml/4 tbsp dry Madeira
900g/2lb can or packet sauerkraut, rinsed
4 tomatoes, peeled and chopped
4 cloves
5cm/2in cinnamon stick
1 bay leaf
2.5ml/½ tsp dill seeds
600ml/1 pint/2½ cups stock
salt and freshly ground black pepper

1 Pour boiling water to completely cover the dried mushrooms and prunes in a bowl. Leave for 30 minutes, then drain well.

2 Cut the pork, venison, chuck steak and *kielbasa* sausage into 2.5cm/1in cubes, then toss together in the flour. Gently fry the onions in the oil for 10 minutes. Remove.

3 Brown the meat in the pan in several batches, for about 5 minutes, or until well browned; remove and set aside. Add the Madeira and simmer for 2–3 minutes, stirring.

4 Return the meat to the pan with the onion, sauerkraut, tomatoes, cloves, cinnamon, bay leaf, dill seeds, mushrooms and prunes. Pour in the stock and season with salt and pepper.

5 Bring to the boil, cover and simmer gently for 1¾–2 hours, or until the meat is very tender. Uncover for the last 20 minutes to let the liquid evaporate, as the stew should be thick. Sprinkle with chopped parsley. Serve immediately with boiled new potatoes, tossed in chopped parsley.

COOK'S TIP

Kielbasa is a garlic-flavoured pork and beef sausage, but any similar type of continental sausage can be used. Use porcini mushrooms, if possible.

Kovbasa

These Ukrainian pork and beef sausages can be made several days ahead and kept refrigerated.

INGREDIENTS

Serves 6

450g/1lb pork, such as shoulder
225g/8oz chuck steak
115g/4oz pork back fat
2 eggs, beaten
30ml/2 tbsp *peperivka* (see *Cook's Tip*)
   or pepper vodka
2.5ml/¹/₂ tsp ground allspice
5ml/1 tsp salt
about 1.75 litres/3 pints/7¹/₂ cups
   chicken stock
fresh parsley, to garnish
mashed potato, to serve

1 Mince the meats and pork back fat together, using the coarse blade of a mincer, then mince half the mixture again, this time using a fine blade.

2 Combine both the meat mixtures with the eggs, *peperivka*, allspice and salt. Check the seasoning by frying a small piece of the mixture, then tasting it. Adjust if necessary.

3 Form the meat mixture into 2 sausages, about 20cm/8in long. Wrap in double buttered muslin and tie securely with string.

4 Bring the stock to a gentle simmer in a large pan. Add the sausages and simmer gently, turning frequently, for 35–40 minutes, or until the juices run clear when the sausages are pierced with a fine skewer.

5 Leave the sausages in the stock for 20 minutes, then remove and leave to cool. Remove the muslin and sauté the sausages in oil to brown them. Garnish with parsley and serve with mashed potato, topped with butter.

— COOK'S TIP —

Spicing whisky with peppers to make *peperivka* is an old tradition in the Ukraine. Add 3 whole cayenne peppers, pricked all over with a fine skewer, to 150ml/¼ pint/ ²/₃ cup whisky or bourbon and leave for at least 48 hours.

Field-roasted Lamb

This unusual recipe, originally for mutton slowly roasted over charcoal, comes from the Russian steppes.

INGREDIENTS

Serves 6
1.75kg/4lb leg of lamb
4 large garlic cloves, cut into slivers
5ml/1 tsp whole peppercorns
300ml/½ pint/1¼ cups natural yogurt
15ml/1 tbsp olive oil
15ml/1 tbsp chopped fresh dill
300ml/½ pint/1¼ cups lamb or
    vegetable stock
30ml/2 tbsp lemon juice
potatoes, spinach and carrots, to serve

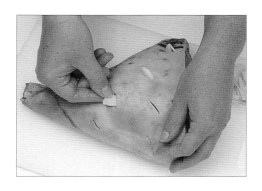

1 Make slits all over the lamb and insert generous slivers of fresh garlic into the slits.

2 Lightly crush the whole peppercorns in a pestle and mortar or rolling pin, if preferred.

3 Tip the yogurt, oil and crushed peppercorns into a bowl, then add the dill and mix together well.

4 Spread the yogurt paste evenly over the lamb. Put the lamb in a glass dish, cover loosely with foil and then refrigerate the lamb for 1–2 days, turning it twice.

5 Transfer the lamb to a roasting tin and let it come back to room temperature. Preheat the oven to 220°C/425°F/Gas 7. Remove the foil. Pour in the stock and lemon juice and cook, uncovered, for 20 minutes.

6 Reduce the oven temperature to 180°C/350°F/Gas 4 and continue roasting for a further 1¼–1½ hours, basting occasionally. Remove from the oven and keep covered in a warm place for 15–20 minutes before carving. Use the juices from the pan to make a gravy and serve with roast potatoes, boiled spinach and baby carrots.

Lamb Plov

Plov is the Russian name for this rice dish popular throughout Eastern Europe, known by different names – *pilau* in Turkey and *pilaf* in the Middle East.

INGREDIENTS

Serves 4

50g/2oz/scant ½ cup raisins
115g/4oz/½ cup stoned prunes
15ml/1 tbsp lemon juice
25g/1oz/2 tbsp butter
1 large onion, chopped
450g/1lb lamb fillet, trimmed and cut into 1cm/½ in cubes
225g/8oz lean minced lamb
2 garlic cloves, crushed
600ml/1 pint/2½ cups lamb or vegetable stock
350g/12oz/scant 2 cups long-grain rice
large pinch of saffron
salt and freshly ground black pepper
sprigs of flat leaf parsley, to garnish

1 Put the raisins and prunes in a small bowl and pour over enough water to cover. Add the lemon juice and leave to soak for at least 1 hour. Drain, then roughly chop the prunes.

2 Meanwhile, heat the butter in a large pan and cook the onion for 5 minutes. Add the lamb fillet, minced lamb and garlic. Fry for 5 minutes, stirring constantly until browned.

3 Pour in 150ml/¼ pint/⅔ cup of the stock. Bring to the boil, then lower the heat, cover and simmer for 1 hour, or until the lamb is tender.

4 Add the remaining stock and bring to the boil. Add the rice and saffron. Stir, then cover and simmer for 15 minutes, or until the rice is tender.

5 Stir in the raisins, chopped prunes, salt and pepper. Heat through for a few minutes, then turn on to a warmed serving dish and garnish with sprigs of flat leaf parsley.

Chicken Bitki

Chicken is one of the most popular meats eaten in Poland. Use guinea fowl to mimic the gamey flavour of Polish chicken.

INGREDIENTS

Makes 12
15g/½oz/1 tbsp butter, melted
115g/4oz flat mushrooms,
    finely chopped
50g/2oz/1 cup fresh white
    breadcrumbs
350g/12oz chicken breasts or guinea
    fowl, minced or finely chopped
2 eggs, separated
1.5ml/¼ tsp grated nutmeg
30ml/2 tbsp plain flour
45ml/3 tbsp oil
salt and freshly ground black pepper
green salad and grated pickled
    beetroot, to serve

1 Melt the butter in a pan and fry the mushrooms for 5 minutes until soft and all the juices have evaporated. Allow to cool.

2 Mix the crumbs, chicken, yolks, nutmeg, salt and pepper and flat mushrooms well.

3 Whisk the egg whites until stiff. Stir half into the chicken mixture, then fold in the remainder.

4 Shape the mixture into 12 even meatballs, about 7.5cm/3in long and 2.5cm/1in wide. Roll in the flour to coat.

5 Heat the oil in a frying pan and fry the *bitki* for 10 minutes, turning until evenly golden brown and cooked through. Serve hot with a green salad and pickled beetroot.

Chicken Kiev

This popular recipe is a modern Russian invention. These deep fried chicken breasts filled with garlic butter should be prepared well in advance to allow time for chilling.

INGREDIENTS

Serves 4
115g/4oz/8 tbsp butter, softened
2 garlic cloves, crushed
finely grated rind of 1 lemon
30ml/2 tbsp chopped fresh tarragon
pinch of freshly grated nutmeg
4 chicken breast fillets with wing
    bones attached, skinned
1 egg, lightly beaten
115g/4oz/2 cups fresh breadcrumbs
oil, for deep frying
salt and freshly ground black pepper
lemon wedges, to garnish
potato wedges, to serve

1 Mix the butter in a bowl with the garlic, lemon rind, tarragon and nutmeg. Season to taste with salt and pepper. Shape the butter into a rectangular block about 5cm/2in long, wrap in foil and chill for 1 hour.

2 Place the chicken, skinned sides down, on a piece of oiled clear film. Cover with a second piece of clear film and gently beat the pieces with a rolling pin until fairly thin.

3 Cut the butter lengthways into four pieces and put one in the centre of each chicken fillet. Fold the edges over the butter and secure with wooden cocktail sticks.

4 Tip the beaten egg and the breadcrumbs into separate small dishes. Dip the chicken pieces first in the beaten egg and then in the breadcrumbs to coat evenly. Dip them a second time in egg and crumbs, then put on a plate and refrigerate for at least 1 hour.

5 Heat the oil in a large pan or deep fat fryer to 180°C/350°F. Deep fry the chicken for 6–8 minutes, or until the chicken is cooked and the coating golden brown and crisp. Drain on kitchen paper and remove the cocktail sticks. Serve hot, garnished with wedges of lemon and potato wedges.

Chicken and Pork Terrine

Serve this delicate Ukrainian pâté with warm, crusty bread.

INGREDIENTS

Serves 6–8

225g/8oz rindless, streaky bacon
375g/13oz boneless chicken
  breast, skinned
15ml/1 tbsp lemon juice
225g/8oz lean minced pork
½ small onion, finely chopped
2 eggs, beaten
30ml/2 tbsp chopped fresh parsley
5ml/1 tsp salt
5ml/1 tsp green peppercorns, crushed
fresh green salad, radishes and lemon
  wedges, to serve

1 Preheat the oven to 160°C/325°F/ Gas 3. Put the bacon on a board and stretch it using the back of a knife so that it can be arranged in over-lapping slices over the base and sides of a 900g/2lb loaf tin.

2 Cut 115g/4oz of the chicken into strips about 10cm/4in long. Sprinkle with lemon juice. Put the rest of the chicken in a food processor or blender with the minced pork and the onion. Process until fairly smooth.

3 Add the eggs, parsley, salt and peppercorns to the meat mixture and process again briefly. Spoon half the mixture into the loaf tin and then level the surface.

4 Arrange the chicken strips on top, then spoon in the remaining meat mixture and smooth the top. Give the tin a couple of sharp taps to knock out any pockets of air.

5 Cover with a piece of oiled foil and put in a roasting tin. Pour in enough hot water to come halfway up the sides of the loaf tin. Bake for about 45–50 minutes, until firm.

6 Allow the terrine to cool in the tin before turning out and chilling. Serve sliced, with a fresh green salad, baby tomatoes and wedges of lemon to squeeze over.

Roast Duckling with Honey

A sweet and sour orange sauce is the perfect foil for this rich-tasting Polish duck recipe, and frying the orange rind intensifies the flavour.

INGREDIENTS

Serves 4
2.25kg/5lb oven-ready duckling
2.5ml/½ tsp ground allspice
1 orange
15ml/1 tbsp sunflower oil
30ml/2 tbsp plain flour
150ml/¼ pint/⅔ cup chicken or
   duck stock
10ml/2 tsp red wine vinegar
15ml/1 tbsp clear honey
salt and freshly ground black pepper
watercress and thinly pared orange
   rind, to serve

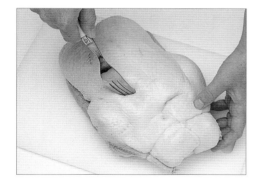

1 Preheat the oven to 220°C/425°F/ Gas 7. Using a fork, pierce the duckling all over, except the breast, so that the fat runs out during cooking.

2 Rub all over the skin of the duckling with allspice and sprinkle with salt and pepper.

3 Put the duckling on a rack over a roasting tin and cook for about 20 minutes. Next reduce the oven temperature to 190°C/375°F/Gas 5 and cook for a further 2 hours.

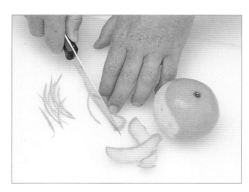

4 Meanwhile, thinly pare the rind from the orange and cut into very fine strips. Heat the oil in a pan and gently fry the orange rind for 2–3 minutes. Squeeze the juice from the orange and set aside.

5 Transfer the duckling to a warmed serving dish and keep warm. Drain off all but 30ml/2 tbsp fat from the tin, sprinkle in the flour and stir well.

6 Stir in the stock, vinegar, honey, orange juice and rind. Bring to the boil, stirring all the time. Simmer for 2–3 minutes. Season the sauce and serve the duckling with watercress and thinly pared orange rind.

FISH

The seas to the north and south and the vast lakes and the rivers that flow across this region provide an abundance of fish, which are cooked in wonderful ways. Russia's most famous export, caviare, comes from the huge sturgeon that swim in the Caspian Sea. The Baltic provides this region with herring, which is served in many guises throughout the year since it is well suited to pickling. However, freshwater fish predominate. These include eel, perch, tench and salmon, but the favourites are pike and carp – always served on feast days.

Pike and Salmon Mousse

When sliced, this light-textured Russian mousse loaf, *Pate iz Shchuki*, reveals a pretty layer of pink salmon. For a special occasion, serve topped with red salmon caviare.

INGREDIENTS

Serves 8

225g/8oz salmon fillets, skinned
600ml/1 pint/2½ cups fish stock
finely grated rind and juice of
½ lemon
900g/2lb pike fillets, skinned
4 egg whites
475ml/16fl oz/2 cups double cream
30ml/2 tbsp chopped fresh dill
salt and freshly ground black pepper
red salmon caviare or dill sprig,
to garnish (optional)

1 Preheat the oven to 180°C/350°F/ Gas 4. Line a 900g/2lb loaf tin with greaseproof paper and brush with oil.

2 Cut the salmon into 5cm/2in strips. Place the stock and lemon juice in a pan and bring to the boil, then turn off the heat. Add the salmon strips, cover and leave for 2 minutes. Remove with a slotted spoon.

3 Cut the pike into cubes and process in a food processor or blender until smooth. Lightly whisk the egg whites with a fork. With the motor running, slowly pour in the egg whites, then the cream. Finally, add the lemon rind, dill and seasoning.

4 Spoon half of the pike mixture into the prepared loaf tin.

5 Arrange the poached salmon strips on top, then carefully spoon in the remaining pike mixture.

6 Cover the loaf tin with foil and put in a roasting tin. Add enough boiling water to come halfway up the sides of the loaf tin. Bake for 45–50 minutes, or until firm.

7 Leave on a wire rack to cool, then chill for at least 3 hours. Turn out on to a serving plate and remove the lining paper. Serve the mousse cut in slices and garnished with red salmon caviare or a sprig of dill, if liked.

Salmon Kulebyaka

A Russian festive dish in which a layer of moist salmon and eggs sits on a bed of buttery dill-flavoured rice, all encased in crisp puff pastry.

INGREDIENTS

Serves 4

50g/2oz/4 tbsp butter
1 small onion, finely chopped
175g/6oz/1 cup cooked long-grain rice
15ml/1 tbsp chopped fresh dill
15ml/1 tbsp lemon juice
450g/1lb puff pastry, defrosted if frozen
450g/1lb salmon fillet, skinned and cut into 5cm/2in pieces
3 eggs, hard-boiled and chopped
beaten egg, for sealing and glazing
salt and freshly ground black pepper
watercress, to garnish

1 Preheat the oven to 200°C/400°F/Gas 6. Melt the butter in a pan, add the finely chopped onion and cook gently for 10 minutes, or until soft.

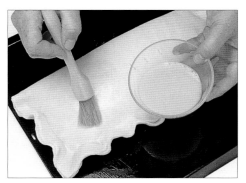

2 Stir in the cooked rice, dill, lemon juice, salt and pepper.

3 Roll out the puff pastry on a lightly floured surface to a 30cm/12in square. Spoon the rice mixture over half the pastry, leaving a 1cm/½in border around the edges.

4 Arrange the salmon on top, then scatter the eggs in between.

5 Brush the pastry edges with egg, fold it over the filling to make a rectangle, pressing the edges together firmly to seal.

6 Carefully lift the pastry on to a lightly oiled baking sheet. Glaze with beaten egg, then pierce the pastry a few times with a skewer to make holes for the steam to escape.

7 Bake on the middle shelf of the oven for 40 minutes, covering with foil after 30 minutes. Leave to cool on the baking sheet, before cutting into slices. Garnish with watercress.

Braised Tench and Vegetables

Freshwater tench is the smallest member of the carp family, with a sweet firm flesh and few bones. In this simple Polish recipe, the combination of vegetables can easily be adapted to suit an individual's taste or seasonal availability.

INGREDIENTS

Serves 4
900g/2lb tench, filleted
   and skinned
15ml/1 tbsp lemon juice
75g/3oz/6 tbsp butter
1 onion, halved and cut into wedges
1 celery stick, sliced
1 carrot, halved lengthways and sliced
115g/4oz/1½ cups small button
   mushrooms, halved
50ml/2fl oz/¼ cup vegetable stock
salt and freshly ground black pepper

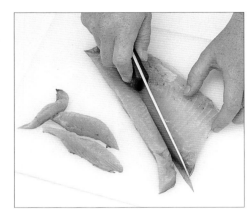

1 Cut the fish fillets into strips about 2.5cm/1in wide. Sprinkle them with the lemon juice and a little salt and pepper and set aside.

2 Melt the butter in a large flameproof casserole and cook the onion wedges for 5 minutes. Add the celery, carrot and mushrooms and cook for a further 2–3 minutes, stirring to coat in the butter.

3 Pour the stock into the pan. Place the fish on top of the vegetables in a single layer. Cover the casserole with a lid and cook over a very low heat for 25–30 minutes, until the fish and vegetables are tender.

VARIATION

Use small carp in this recipe if liked. Carp has a slightly muddier flavour.

Plaice in Polish Sauce

This sauce is Polish only in name, not in origin. A mixture of recipes, it is a quick and simple sauce to prepare, that goes well with any poached, grilled or steamed fish.

INGREDIENTS

Serves 4
4 plaice fillets, about 225g/8oz each
75g/3oz/6 tbsp butter
2 eggs, hard-boiled and
   finely chopped
30ml/2 tbsp chopped fresh dill
15ml/1 tbsp lemon juice
salt and freshly ground black pepper
lemon slices, to garnish
boiled baby carrots, to serve

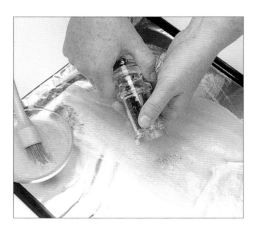

1 Put the fish, skin side down, on a sheet of greased foil on a grill rack. Melt the butter in a small pan and brush a little over the fish. Season with salt and pepper.

2 Grill the fish under a moderate heat for 8–10 minutes, or until just cooked. Transfer to a warmed plate.

3 Add the eggs, dill and lemon juice to the melted butter in the pan. Heat gently for 1 minute. Pour over the fish just before serving. Garnish with lemon slices and serve with boiled baby carrots.

Fish Babka

This fish pudding is lightened with egg whites, giving it a soufflé-like texture. It is much more stable, however, and can be turned out to serve.

INGREDIENTS

Serves 4
350g/12oz white fish fillets, skinned and cut into 2.5cm/1in cubes
50g/2oz white bread, cut into 1cm/½in cubes
250ml/8fl oz/1 cup milk
25g/1oz/2 tbsp butter
1 small onion, finely chopped
3 eggs, separated
1.5ml/¼ tsp grated nutmeg
salt and freshly ground black pepper
30ml/2 tbsp chopped fresh dill, plus extra to garnish
sliced courgettes and carrots, to serve

1 Preheat the oven to 180°C/350°F/ Gas 4. Base-line with greaseproof paper and butter a 1.5 litre/2½ pint/ 6¼ cup ovenproof dish.

2 Place the fish cubes in a bowl. Add the bread, then sprinkle over the milk and leave to soak while you cook the chopped onion.

3 Melt the butter in a small pan and fry the onion for 10 minutes, until soft. Cool for a few minutes, then add to the fish and bread with the egg yolks, nutmeg, dill, salt and pepper. Mix well.

4 Whisk the egg whites in a large bowl until stiff, then gently fold into the fish mixture.

5 Spoon the mixture into the dish. Cover with buttered foil and bake for 45 minutes, or until set.

6 Allow to stand for 5 minutes, then spoon out. Alternatively, loosen with a knife; turn out, remove the paper and cut into wedges. Garnish with dill and serve with courgettes and carrots.

Muscovite Solyanka

This layered fish and vegetable bake has the same name as one of Russia's classic soups. The name reflects the prevalent "sourness" of the ingredients.

INGREDIENTS

Serves 4
675g/1½lb eel, skinned and boned
900ml/1½ pints/3¾ cups fish or
  vegetable stock
1.2 litres/2 pints/5 cups water
450g/1lb/4 cups shredded
  white cabbage
50g/2oz/4 tbsp butter
1 large onion, chopped
2 pickled cucumbers, sliced
12 green olives
15ml/1 tbsp capers, drained
75g/3oz/1½ cups fresh white
  breadcrumbs
salt and freshly ground black pepper

1 Cut the eel into large pieces. Bring the stock to a gentle simmer in a large pan, add the eel and cook for 4 minutes. Remove with a slotted spoon. Reserve 150ml/¼ pint/⅔ cup of the stock and set aside, leaving the remaining stock in the pan.

2 Pour the water into the pan of stock. Bring to the boil, then add the cabbage. Simmer for 2 minutes, then strain well.

3 Melt half of the butter in the pan. Fry the onion for 5 minutes.

4 Stir in the strained cabbage and reserved stock, then bring to the boil. Cover with a tight-fitting lid and cook over a low heat for 1 hour, until tender. Season with salt and pepper.

5 Preheat the oven to 200°C/400°F/ Gas 6. Spoon half the cabbage into a baking dish. Top with the eel and the cucumbers. Spoon over the remaining cabbage and any remaining stock.

6 Scatter the olives, capers and the breadcrumbs over the top. Melt the remaining butter and drizzle over the top. Bake for 25–30 minutes, or until lightly browned. Garnish with parsley sprigs and serve with boiled potatoes.

Rolled Fish Fillets

Whiting or sea perch can also be used in this dish. Their delicate flavour is complemented by the lemon and thyme.

INGREDIENTS

Serves 4
8 sole fillets, about 200g/7oz, skinned
45ml/3 tbsp olive oil
15ml/1 tbsp lemon juice
25g/1oz/2 tbsp butter
175g/6oz/2 cups button mushrooms, very finely chopped
4 anchovy fillets, finely chopped
5ml/1 tsp chopped fresh thyme, plus extra to garnish
2 eggs, beaten
115g/4oz/2 cups white breadcrumbs
oil, for deep frying
salt and freshly ground black pepper
grilled chicory, to serve

1 Lay the fish fillets in a single layer in a glass dish. Mix together the oil and lemon juice and sprinkle over. Cover with clear film and marinate in the refrigerator for at least 1 hour.

2 Melt the butter in a pan and gently fry the mushrooms for 5 minutes, until tender and all the juices have evaporated. Stir in the chopped anchovies, thyme, salt and pepper.

3 Divide the mixture equally and spread evenly over the fish. Roll up and secure with cocktail sticks.

———— COOK'S TIP ————

To skin the fillets, slice the flesh away from the skin using a sharp knife. Keep the knife parallel to the fish and the skin taut.

4 Dip each fish roll in beaten egg, then in breadcrumbs to coat. Repeat this process. Heat the oil to 180°C/350°F/Gas 4.

5 Deep fry in 2 batches for 4–5 minutes, or until well browned and cooked through. Drain on kitchen paper. Remove the cocktail sticks and sprinkle with thyme. Serve with grilled chicory.

Carp with Green Horseradish Sauce

Carp is a freshwater fish much used in Polish cooking, and it is traditional Christmas fare.

INGREDIENTS

Serves 4
675g/1½lb carp, skinned and filleted
45ml/3 tbsp plain flour
1 egg, beaten
115g/4oz/2 cups fresh white breadcrumbs
sunflower oil, for frying
salt and freshly ground black pepper
lemon wedges, to serve

For the sauce
15g/½oz fresh horseradish, finely grated
pinch of salt
150ml/¼ pint/⅔ cup double cream
1 bunch of watercress, trimmed and finely chopped
30ml/2 tbsp snipped fresh chives
2 eggs, hard-boiled and finely chopped (optional)

1 Cut the fish into thin strips, about 6cm/2½in long by 1cm/½in thick. Season the flour with salt and pepper. Dip the strips of fish in the flour, then in the beaten egg and finally in the breadcrumbs.

2 Heat 1cm/½in of oil in a frying pan. Fry the fish in batches for 3–4 minutes, until golden brown. Drain on kitchen paper and keep warm until all the strips are cooked.

3 For the sauce, put the horseradish, salt, cream and watercress in a small pan. Bring to the boil and simmer for 2 minutes. Stir in the chives and eggs, if using. Serve the sauce with the fish.

Baked Cod with Horseradish Sauce

Baking fish in a sauce keeps it moist. In this Ukrainian recipe, a second, tangy sauce is served alongside for added flavour.

INGREDIENTS

Serves 4
4 thick cod fillets or steaks
15ml/1 tbsp lemon juice
25g/1oz/2 tbsp butter
25g/1oz/¼ cup plain flour, sifted
150ml/¼ pint/⅔ cup milk
150ml/¼ pint/⅔ cup fish stock
salt and freshly ground black pepper
parsley sprigs, to garnish
potato wedges and chopped spring
  onions, fried, to serve

For the horseradish sauce
30ml/2 tbsp tomato purée
30ml/2 tbsp grated fresh horseradish
150ml/¼ pint/⅔ cup soured cream

1 Preheat the oven to 180°C/350°F/ Gas 4. Place the fish in a buttered ovenproof dish in a single layer. Sprinkle with lemon juice.

2 Melt the butter in a small heavy-based pan. Stir in the flour and cook for 3–4 minutes until lightly golden. Stir to stop the flour sticking to the pan. Remove from the heat.

3 Gradually whisk the milk, and then the stock, into the flour mixture. Season with salt and pepper. Bring to the boil, stirring, and simmer for 3 minutes, still stirring.

4 Pour the sauce over the fish and bake for 20–25 minutes, depending on the thickness. Check by inserting a skewer in the thickest part: the flesh should be opaque.

5 For the horseradish sauce, blend the tomato purée and horseradish with the soured cream in a small pan. Slowly bring to the boil, stirring, and then simmer for 1 minute.

6 Pour the horseradish sauce into a serving bowl and serve alongside the fish. Serve the fish hot. Garnish with the parsley sprigs and serve with the potato wedges and fried chopped spring onions.

Glazed Pike-perch

This Russian fish dish, with its glistening aspic coating, makes an impressive centrepiece for a formal occasion.

Ingredients

Serves 8–10

2.25–2.75kg/5–6lb whole pike-perch
30ml/2 tbsp sunflower oil
2 bay leaves
8 whole peppercorns
1 lemon, sliced
300ml/½ pint/1¼ cups white wine
25g/1oz sachet aspic jelly
2 cucumbers, halved and thinly sliced
salt and freshly ground black pepper
dill sprigs and lemon wedges,
   to garnish
mayonnaise, to serve

1 Wash the pike-perch under cold running water. Snip off the fins with sharp scissors. Season the inside of the fish with salt and pepper. Brush the skin with the oil to protect it from the heat during cooking.

2 Put the fish on the trivet of a fish kettle or on a rack in a large roasting tin. Add the bay leaves, peppercorns and lemon slices. Pour over the wine and enough water to cover.

3 Cover with a lid or a piece of oiled foil. Bring to the boil and simmer very gently for 10 minutes. Turn off the heat and leave the pike-perch to cool with the lid still on. When cool peel the skin off the fish, leaving the head and tail intact.

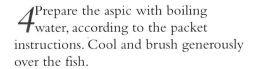

4 Prepare the aspic with boiling water, according to the packet instructions. Cool and brush generously over the fish.

5 Arrange the cucumber slices over the fish, then brush again with aspic. Allow to set before serving, garnished with dill sprigs and lemon wedges.

> ——— Cook's Tip ———
>
> A whole fresh salmon or salmon trout can be cooked in exactly the same way.

VEGETABLES, GRAINS AND PASTA

Served on their own or as an accompaniment, vegetables in Russia, Poland and the Ukraine reflect the cold climate. Cabbage, beetroot, swede and turnip are the staples, often preserved by salting or pickling. Mushrooms are popular, too, since huge forests cover much of the region and gathering them is a favourite pastime. Potatoes also feature, particularly in Polish cooking, although grains, especially buckwheat, rye and barley, are more widely eaten. Surprisingly, stuffed pasta is traditional, usually with meat or cheese fillings.

Potato Cakes

Although not as widely used as cereals, potatoes feature often in Polish recipes. They were introduced during the reign of Jan Sobieski, in the 17th century.

INGREDIENTS

Serves 4

450g/1lb potatoes, peeled and cut into large chunks
25g/1oz/2 tbsp butter
1 small onion, chopped
45ml/3 tbsp soured cream
2 egg yolks
25g/1oz/¼ cup plain flour
1 egg, beaten
25g/1oz/½ cup fresh white breadcrumbs
salt and freshly ground black pepper

1 Preheat the oven to 180°C/350°F/ Gas 4. Cook the potatoes in a pan of boiling salted water for 20 minutes, or until tender. Drain well and mash. Allow to cool for a few minutes. Meanwhile, melt the butter in a small pan and fry the onion for 10 minutes, until soft.

2 Stir the butter and onion into the mashed potato and then mix in the cream and egg yolks.

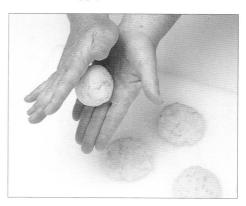

3 Sift the flour over the potato mixture, then mix it in well. Season with plenty of salt and pepper. Shape into rounds, then flatten slightly to make about 16 "doughnuts" 6cm/ 2½in across.

4 Place the "doughnuts" on a lightly oiled baking sheet and brush with beaten egg. Sprinkle the tops with breadcrumbs. Bake for 30 minutes, or until browned.

Pampushki

When these crunchy Russian potato dumplings are split open, a tasty curd cheese and chive filling is revealed.

INGREDIENTS

Serves 4
675g/1½lb potatoes, peeled
225g/8oz/2⅔ cups cooked
  mashed potato
2.5ml/½ tsp salt
75g/3oz/scant ½ cup curd cheese
30ml/2 tbsp snipped fresh chives
freshly ground black pepper
oil, for deep frying

1 Coarsely grate the raw potatoes and squeeze out as much water as possible. Put them in a bowl with the mashed potato, salt and black pepper. Mix together. In another bowl, mix the curd cheese and chives together.

2 Using a spoon and your fingers, scoop up a portion of the potato mixture, slightly smaller than an egg, and then flatten to a circle.

3 Put 5ml/1 tsp of the cheese filling into the middle, then fold over the edges and pinch to seal. Repeat with remaining potato and cheese mixtures, to make about 12 dumplings.

4 Heat the oil to 170°C/340°F. Deep fry the dumplings for 10 minutes, or until deep brown and crisp. Drain on kitchen paper and serve hot.

--- COOK'S TIP ---

Pampushki are traditionally cooked in stock or water and served with soup. If you prefer to poach them, add 15ml/1 tbsp plain flour and 1 beaten egg to the mixture and poach the dumplings for 20 minutes.

Galushki

One of the most popular Ukrainian dishes, *galushki* are pieces of a pasta-like dough, cooked in milk or stock. Healthy and filling, they can be made from wheat flour, buckwheat flour, semolina or potatoes.

Ingredients

Serves 4

225g/8oz/2 cups plain flour
1.5ml/¼ tsp salt
25g/1oz/2 tbsp butter, melted
2 eggs, beaten
1 vegetable stock cube
115g/4oz lardons or smoked streaky
  bacon, rinded and chopped,
  to serve

1 Sift the flour and salt into a bowl. Make a well in the centre. Add the butter and eggs and mix to a dough.

2 Knead on a lightly floured surface until smooth. Wrap in clear film and leave to rest for 30 minutes. Roll out on a lightly floured surface until 1cm/½in thick, and cut into 2cm/¾in squares using a sharp knife or a pastry wheel. Leave to dry on a floured dish towel for 30 minutes.

3 Crumble the stock cube into a pan of gently boiling water. Add the *galushki* and simmer for 10 minutes, or until cooked. Drain well.

4 Meanwhile, dry fry the lardons or bacon in a non-stick frying pan for 5 minutes, until brown and crispy. Serve scattered over the *galushki*.

Cheese Dumplings

Easily prepared, dumplings are common additions to soups throughout the Ukraine. They are also served with meats and on their own as a simple supper.

Ingredients

Serves 4

115g/4oz/1 cup self-raising flour
25g/1oz/2 tbsp butter
25g/1oz/⅓ cup crumbled feta, dry
  brinza (sheep's milk cheese), or a
  mixture of Caerphilly and Parmesan
30ml/2 tbsp chopped fresh herbs
60ml/4 tbsp cold water
salt and freshly ground black pepper
parsley sprigs, to garnish

For the topping

40g/1½oz/3 tbsp butter
50g/2oz/1 cup slightly dry white
  breadcrumbs

1 Sift the flour into a bowl. Rub in the butter until the mixture resembles fine breadcrumbs.

2 Stir the cheese and herbs into the mixture. Season with salt and pepper. Add the cold water and mix to a firm dough; then shape into 12 balls.

3 Bring a pan of salted water to the boil. Add the dumplings, cover and gently simmer for 20 minutes, until light and fluffy.

4 For the topping, melt the butter in a frying pan. Add the breadcrumbs and cook for 2–3 minutes, until the crumbs are golden and crisp. Remove the dumplings with a slotted spoon and sprinkle with breadcrumbs. Serve garnished with parsley sprigs.

Drachena

A Russian cross between an omelette and a pancake, this is a savoury *drachena,* but it is often served as a dessert by leaving out the vegetables and sweetening with sugar or honey.

INGREDIENTS

Serves 2–3

15ml/1 tbsp olive oil
1 bunch spring onions, sliced
1 garlic clove, crushed
4 tomatoes, peeled, seeded
  and chopped
45ml/3 tbsp wholemeal rye flour
60ml/4 tbsp milk
150ml/¹/₄ pint/²/₃ cup soured cream
4 eggs, beaten
30ml/2 tbsp chopped fresh parsley
25g/1oz/2 tbsp butter, melted
salt and freshly ground black pepper
green salad, to serve

1 Preheat the oven to 180°C/350°F/ Gas 4. Heat the oil in a frying pan and gently cook the spring onions for 3 minutes. Add the garlic and cook for 1 more minute, or until the spring onions are soft.

2 Sprinkle the spring onions and garlic into the base of a lightly greased shallow 20cm/8in ovenproof dish and scatter over the tomatoes.

3 Mix the flour to a smooth paste in a bowl with the milk. Gradually add the soured cream, then mix with the eggs. Stir in the parsley and melted butter. Season with salt and pepper.

4 Pour the egg mixture over the vegetables. Bake in the oven for 40–45 minutes, or until hardly any liquid seeps out when a knife is pushed into the middle.

5 Run a knife around the edge of the dish to loosen, then cut into wedges and serve immediately with a fresh green salad.

Braised Barley and Vegetables

One of the oldest of cultivated cereals, pot barley has a nutty flavour and slightly chewy texture. It makes a warming and filling dish when combined with root vegetables.

INGREDIENTS

Serves 4

225g/8oz/1 cup pearl or pot barley
30ml/2 tbsp sunflower oil
1 large onion, chopped
2 celery sticks, sliced
2 carrots, halved lengthways and sliced
225g/8oz swede or turnip, cut into 2cm/³⁄₄ in cubes
225g/8oz potatoes, cut into 2cm/³⁄₄ in cubes
475ml/16fl oz/2 cups vegetable stock
salt and freshly ground black pepper
celery leaves, to garnish

1 Put the barley in a measuring jug and add water to reach the 600ml/1 pint/2¹⁄₂ cup mark. Leave to soak in a cool place for at least 4 hours or, preferably, overnight.

2 Heat the oil in a large pan and fry the onion for 5 minutes. Add the sliced celery and carrots and cook for 3–4 minutes, or until the onion is starting to brown.

3 Add the barley and its soaking liquid to the pan. Then add the swede or turnip, potato and stock to the barley. Season with salt and pepper. Bring to the boil, then reduce the heat and cover the pan.

4 Simmer for 40 minutes, or until most of the stock has been absorbed and the barley is tender. Stir occasionally towards the end of cooking to prevent the barley from sticking to the base of the pan. Serve, garnished with celery leaves.

Buckwheat Kasha

Kasha is a type of Russian porridge, made from a variety of grains including wheat, barley, millet and oats. The most popular is buckwheat, which has a distinctive nutty flavour.

INGREDIENTS

Serves 4

175g/6oz/scant 1 cup buckwheat
750ml/1¼ pints/3 cups boiling stock
25g/1oz/2 tbsp butter
pinch of freshly grated nutmeg
115g/4oz smoked streaky bacon, rinded and chopped
salt and freshly ground black pepper

1 Dry fry the buckwheat in a non-stick frying pan for 2 minutes, or until very lightly toasted. Add the stock.

COOK'S TIP

Buckwheat *kasha* is equally good with the addition of fried mushrooms and makes an excellent stuffing for roast chicken. Buckwheat is often sold already roasted, in which case there is no need to dry fry it before adding the stock.

2 Simmer very gently for 15–20 minutes, stirring occasionally to prevent it sticking. When almost dry, remove from the heat.

3 Add the butter to the buckwheat and season with nutmeg, salt and pepper. Cover the pan with a lid and leave to stand for 5 minutes.

4 Meanwhile, dry fry the bacon in a non-stick pan for 5 minutes, until lightly browned and crispy. Sprinkle over the kasha before serving.

Carters' Millet

This dish was originally cooked over an open fire by carters who travelled across the steppes of southern Ukraine.

INGREDIENTS

Serves 4

225g/8oz/scant 1¼ cups millet
600ml/1 pint/2½ cups vegetable stock
115g/4oz lardons or smoked streaky bacon, rinded and chopped
15ml/1 tbsp olive oil
1 small onion, thinly sliced
225g/8oz/3 cups small field mushrooms, sliced
15ml/1 tbsp chopped fresh mint
salt and freshly ground black pepper

1 Rinse the millet in a sieve under cold running water. Put in a pan with the stock, bring to the boil and simmer, covered, for 30 minutes, until the stock has been absorbed.

2 Dry fry the bacon in a non-stick pan for 5 minutes, or until brown and crisp. Remove and set aside.

3 Add the oil to the pan and cook the onion and mushrooms for 10 minutes, until beginning to brown.

4 Add the bacon, onion and mushrooms to the millet. Stir in the mint and season with salt and pepper. Heat gently for 1–2 minutes before serving.

Beetroot Casserole

This Russian vegetarian casserole can be served as a light meal in itself. Its sweet and sour flavour also makes it an ideal dish to serve with roasted chicken or game.

INGREDIENTS

Serves 4
50g/2oz/4 tbsp butter
1 onion, chopped
2 garlic cloves, crushed
675g/1½lb uncooked beetroot, peeled
2 large carrots, peeled
½ lemon
115g/4oz/1½ cups button mushrooms
300ml/½ pint/1¼ cups
  vegetable stock
2 bay leaves
15ml/1 tbsp chopped fresh mint, plus
  sprigs to garnish (optional)
salt and freshly ground black pepper

For the hot dressing
150ml/¼ pint/⅔ cup soured cream
2.5ml/½ tsp paprika, plus extra
  to garnish

1 Melt the butter in a non-aluminium pan and gently fry the onion and garlic for 5 minutes. Meanwhile, dice the beetroot and carrot. Finely grate the rind and squeeze the juice of the ½ lemon. Add the beetroot, carrots and mushrooms and fry for 5 minutes.

— COOK'S TIP —

Wear clean rubber or plastic gloves to avoid staining your hands when preparing beetroot. Cooking beetroot in aluminium pans may cause discoloration of pan and food.

2 Pour in the stock with the lemon rind and bay leaves. Season with salt and pepper. Bring to the boil, turn down the heat, cover and simmer for 1 hour, or until the vegetables are soft.

3 Turn off the heat and stir in the lemon juice and chopped mint, if using. Leave the pan to stand, covered, for 5 minutes, to develop the flavours.

4 Meanwhile, for the dressing, gently heat the soured cream and paprika in a small pan, stirring all the time, until bubbling. Transfer the beetroot mixture to a serving bowl, then spoon over the soured cream. Garnish with sprigs of mint and extra paprika, if liked, and serve.

Uszka

Uszka, meaning "little ears", are plump mushroom dumplings, traditionally served in Poland with clear soups. They are also delicious on their own, tossed in a little melted butter and chopped fresh herbs.

INGREDIENTS

Makes 20
75g/3oz/²⁄₃ cup plain flour
pinch of salt
30ml/2 tbsp chopped fresh parsley
1 egg yolk
40ml/2½ tbsp cold water
fresh parsley, to garnish
clear soup or melted herb butter,
  to serve

For the filling
25g/1oz/2 tbsp butter
½ small onion, very finely chopped
50g/2oz/1 cup mushrooms,
  finely chopped
1 egg white
15ml/1 tbsp dried white breadcrumbs
salt and freshly ground black pepper

1 Sift the flour and salt into a bowl. Add the chopped parsley, egg yolk and water and mix to a dough. Lightly knead the dough on a floured surface until smooth.

2 To make the filling, melt the butter in a pan. Add the onion and mushrooms and fry over a low heat for 10 minutes, or until the onion is very soft. Leave to cool.

3 Lightly whisk the egg white in a clean bowl with a fork. Add 15ml/ 1 tbsp of the egg white to the mushrooms, together with the dried breadcrumbs, salt and pepper. Mix together well.

4 Roll out the dough very thinly on a floured surface. Cut into 5cm/2in squares using a sharp knife or a pastry wheel, then lightly brush with the remaining egg white.

5 Spoon 2.5ml/½ tsp of mushroom mixture on to each square. Fold the dough in half to make a triangle, then pinch the outer edges together to seal them.

6 Bring a pan of boiling salted water or stock to a brisk boil. Gently drop in the dumplings a few at a time and simmer for 5 minutes. Drain and add to a clear soup or toss in melted herb butter and serve.

Cucumber Salad

Salting the cucumber draws out some of the moisture, thereby making it firmer. Make sure you rinse it thoroughly before using or the salad will be too salty. This popular Ukrainian dish is an ideal summer accompaniment to a main meal.

INGREDIENTS

Serves 6–8
2 cucumbers, decorated with a
   cannelle knife and thinly sliced
5ml/1 tsp salt
45ml/3 tbsp chopped fresh dill
15ml/1 tbsp white wine vinegar
150ml/¼ pint/⅔ cup soured cream
freshly ground black pepper
1 dill sprig, to garnish

1 Put the cucumber in a sieve or colander set over a bowl and sprinkle with the salt. Leave for 1 hour to drain. Rinse the cucumber well under cold running water, then pat dry with kitchen paper.

2 Put the slices of cucumber in a bowl, add the chopped dill and mix everything together well.

3 In another bowl, stir the vinegar into the soured cream and season the mixture with pepper.

4 Pour the soured cream over the cucumber and chill for 1 hour before turning into a serving dish. Garnish with a sprig of dill and serve.

Grated Beetroot and Celery Salad

Raw beetroot has a lovely crunchy texture. Here in this Russian salad, its flavour is brought out by marinating it in a cider dressing.

INGREDIENTS

Serves 4–6
450g/1lb uncooked beetroot, peeled
   and grated
4 celery sticks, finely chopped
30ml/2 tbsp apple juice
fresh herbs, to garnish

For the dressing
45ml/3 tbsp sunflower oil
15ml/1 tbsp cider vinegar
4 spring onions, finely sliced
30ml/2 tbsp chopped fresh parsley
salt and freshly ground black pepper

1 Toss the beetroot, celery and apple juice together in a bowl to mix.

2 Put all the ingredients for the dressing in a small bowl and whisk with a fork until well blended. Stir half into the beetroot mixture.

3 Drizzle the remaining dressing over the top. Allow the salad to marinate for at least 2 hours before serving, for the fullest flavour. Garnish with fresh herbs.

DESSERTS AND BAKES

Russians, Ukrainians and Poles all have a sweet tooth and this is reflected in the vast number and variety of desserts, cakes, pastries and breads. Special occasions are often marked with particular confections, such as Russian Paskha and Polish Babka. Honey and nuts are plentiful and feature in many sweet dishes. Other popular flavourings are cinnamon, cloves and cardamom, as well as candied fruits, vanilla and lemon peel. Fruit, especially orchard and soft fruit, can be of exceptionally high quality.

Kulich

Kulich is served only at Easter in Russia, often instead of bread. Slice in rounds from the top, with the first slice kept as a lid.

INGREDIENTS

Serves 4
500g/1¼lb/5 cups strong white flour
pinch of salt
5ml/1 tsp ground cinnamon
75g/3oz/scant ½ cup caster sugar
50g/2oz/scant ½ cup raisins
50g/2oz/⅓ cup mixed peel
50g/2oz/⅓ cup almonds, chopped
7g/¼oz sachet easy-blend
   dried yeast
300ml/½ pint/1¼ cups milk
50g/2oz/4 tbsp butter
1 egg, beaten
jam, to serve (optional)

For the icing
115g/4oz/1 cup icing sugar
15ml/1 tbsp lemon juice

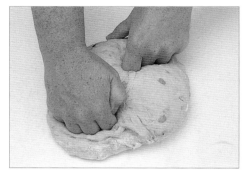

1 Sift the flour, salt and cinnamon into a large bowl. Stir in the sugar, raisins, mixed peel, almonds and dried yeast. Make a well in the centre.

2 Gently heat the milk and butter in a pan until melted. Allow to cool until tepid. Reserve 5ml/1 tsp of the beaten egg for glazing, then add the remainder to the dry ingredients with the milk and butter. Mix well to form a soft dough.

3 Knead the dough on a lightly floured surface for 10 minutes, or until smooth and elastic. Place in a clean bowl, cover with a damp cloth and leave in a warm place to rise for about 1 hour, or until doubled in size.

4 Preheat the oven to 190°C/375°F/ Gas 5. Grease and line a tall cylindrical tin or a deep 20cm/8in round cake tin with greaseproof paper. Turn the dough out and knead again until smooth. Place in the prepared tin, cover with oiled clear film and leave in a warm place until it has risen almost to the top of the tin.

5 Discard the cling film. Brush the top with the reserved egg. Bake for 50–55 minutes, or until a fine skewer inserted into the middle comes out clean. Cover with foil if the *kulich* begins to brown too much. Turn out on to a wire rack to cool.

6 For the icing, sift the icing sugar into a bowl. Add the lemon juice and mix to make a thick icing. Drizzle over the top of the *kulich* and leave to set. Spread with jam, if liked.

Paskha

Paskha is the Russian word for Easter and the name given to this rich curd cheese and candied fruit dessert, which celebrates the end of Lent. Traditionally, it is made in a pyramid-shaped wooden mould with the imprint of the Orthodox cross, but a clean, plastic flowerpot works equally well.

INGREDIENTS

Serves 6–8
115g/4oz/½ cup candied
   fruit, chopped
50g/2oz/scant ½ cup raisins
finely grated rind and juice of 1 lemon
5ml/1 tsp vanilla essence
675g/1½lb/3 cups curd cheese
25g/1oz/2 tbsp unsalted butter
150ml/¼ pint/⅔ cup soured cream
50g/2oz/¼ cup caster sugar
50g/2oz/¼ cup clear honey
50g/2oz/⅓ cup blanched
   almonds, chopped
candied fruits, lemon rind, angelica
   and honey, to decorate

1 Put the candied fruit, raisins, lemon rind and juice and vanilla essence in a small bowl. Stir, then cover and leave to soak for 1 hour.

COOK'S TIP

If preferred, drain the mixture for 1 hour in a muslin-lined sieve, before spooning into the lined pudding basin.

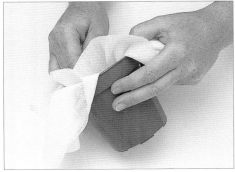

2 Meanwhile, line a 1.5 litre/ 2½ pint/6¼ cup plastic flowerpot with a double layer of muslin, allowing the edges to overhang the pot.

3 Put the cheese, butter and soured cream in a mixing bowl and beat until well blended. Add the sugar, honey, blanched almonds and soaked fruits and mix well.

4 Spoon the mixture into the lined flowerpot and fold the edges of the muslin into the middle. Cover with a small plate or saucer that just fits inside the flowerpot, then top with a 450g/ 1lb weight. Stand the flowerpot on a plate and refrigerate overnight.

5 Unfold the muslin, turn the paskha out on to a plate, then remove the muslin. Before serving, decorate with lemon rind, candied fruit and angelica, and drizzle with honey.

Polish Honey Cake

Many Eastern European cakes, like this Polish *Tort Orzechowy*, are sweetened with honey and made with ground nuts and breadcrumbs instead of flour, which gives them a delicious, rich, moist texture.

INGREDIENTS

Serves 12

15g/½oz/1 tbsp unsalted butter, melted and cooled

115g/4oz/2 cups slightly dry fine white breadcrumbs

175g/6oz/¾ cup set honey, plus extra to serve

50g/2oz/¼ cup soft light brown sugar

4 eggs, separated

115g/4oz/1 cup hazelnuts, chopped and toasted, plus extra to decorate

1 Preheat the oven to 180°C/350°F/ Gas 4. Brush a 1.75 litre/3 pint/ 7½ cup fluted brioche tin with the melted butter. Sprinkle with 15g/½oz/ ¼ cup of the breadcrumbs.

— COOK'S TIP —

The cake will rise during cooking and sink slightly as it cools – this is quite normal.

2 Put the honey in a large bowl, set over a pan of barely simmering water. When the honey liquifies, add the sugar and egg yolks. Whisk until light and frothy. Remove from the heat.

3 Mix the remaining breadcrumbs with the hazelnuts and fold into the egg yolk and honey mixture. Whisk the egg whites in a separate bowl, until stiff, then gently fold in to the other ingredients, half at a time.

4 Spoon the mixture into the tin. Bake for 40–45 minutes, until golden brown. Leave to cool in the tin for 5 minutes, then turn out on to a wire rack to cool. Scatter over nuts and drizzle with extra honey to serve.

Baked Coffee Custards

Unlike the Russians and Ukrainians, the Polish have a passion for coffee and use it in many of their desserts.

INGREDIENTS

Serves 4
25g/1oz/6 tbsp finely ground coffee
300ml/½ pint/1¼ cups milk
150ml/¼ pint/⅔ cup single cream
2 eggs, beaten
30ml/2 tbsp caster sugar
whipped cream and cocoa powder,
  to decorate

1 Preheat the oven to 190ºC/375ºF/ Gas 5. Put the ground coffee in a jug. Heat the milk in a pan until it is nearly boiling. Pour over the coffee and leave to stand for 5 minutes.

2 Strain the coffee-flavoured milk back into the pan. Add the cream and heat again until nearly boiling.

3 Beat the eggs and sugar in a bowl. Pour the hot coffee-flavoured milk into the bowl, whisking all the time. Strain into the rinsed jug.

4 Pour the mixture into 4 × 150ml/ ¼ pint/⅔ cup ramekins. Cover each with a piece of foil.

5 Stand the ramekins in a roasting tin and pour in enough hot water to come halfway up the sides of the ramekins. Bake for 40 minutes, or until lightly set.

6 Remove the ramekins from the roasting tin and allow to cool. Chill for 2 hours. Decorate with a swirl of whipped cream and a sprinkle of cocoa powder, if liked, before serving.

Tort Migdalowy

Almonds are in plentiful supply in Poland and are used in both sweet and savoury dishes. Here they are roasted, giving this coffee-cream-filled sponge a rich and nutty flavour.

INGREDIENTS

Serves 8–10

75g/3oz/½ cup blanched almonds
225g/8oz/1 cup butter, softened
225g/8oz/generous 1 cup caster sugar
4 eggs, beaten
150g/5oz/1¼ cups self-raising flour, sifted

For the icing

175g/6oz/1 cup blanched almonds
40g/1½oz/9 tbsp ground coffee
75ml/5 tbsp near-boiling water
150g/5oz/¾ cup caster sugar
90ml/6 tbsp water
3 egg yolks
225g/8oz/1 cup unsalted butter

1 Preheat the oven to 190°C/375°F/ Gas 5. Lightly grease and base-line 3 × 18cm/7in round cake tins with greaseproof paper.

2 Put the blanched almonds on a baking sheet and roast in the oven for 7 minutes, or until golden brown.

3 Allow to cool, then transfer to a processor or a blender and process until fine.

4 Cream the butter and sugar together in a bowl until pale and fluffy. Gradually add the eggs, a little at a time, beating well after each addition. Fold in the ground roasted almonds and the flour .

5 Divide the cake mixture evenly between the 3 prepared tins and bake for 25–30 minutes, until well risen and firm to the touch, swapping the position of the top and bottom cakes halfway through cooking. Turn out and cool on a wire rack.

6 For the icing, put the blanched almonds in a bowl and pour over enough boiling water to cover. Leave until cold, then drain the almonds and cut each one lengthways into 4 or 5 slivers with a sharp knife. Roast on a baking sheet for 6–8 minutes.

7 Put the ground coffee in a jug, spoon over the water and leave to stand. Gently heat the sugar and 90ml/ 6 tbsp water in a small heavy-based pan until dissolved. Simmer for 3 minutes, until the temperature reaches 107°C/ 225°F on a sugar thermometer.

8 Put the egg yolks into a bowl and pour over the syrup in a thin stream, whisking all the time until very thick. Cream the butter until soft, then gradually beat the egg mixture into it.

9 Strain the coffee through a sieve and beat into the icing. Use two-thirds to sandwich the cakes together. Spread the remainder over the top and press in the almond slivers.

Raisin Cheesecake

Cheesecakes were originally baked rather than set with gelatine. This Ukrainian dessert is an Easter speciality.

INGREDIENTS

Serves 8
115g/4oz/1 cup plain flour
50g/2oz/4 tbsp butter
15ml/1 tbsp caster sugar
25g/1oz/¼ cup almonds, very finely chopped
30ml/2 tbsp cold water
15ml/1 tbsp icing sugar, for dusting

For the filling
115g/4oz/8 tbsp butter
150g/5oz/¾ cup caster sugar
5ml/1 tsp vanilla essence
3 eggs, beaten
25g/1oz/¼ cup plain flour, sifted
400g/14oz/1¾ cups curd cheese
grated rind and juice of 2 lemons
65g/2½ oz/½ cup raisins

1 Sift the flour into a bowl. Rub in the butter, until the mixture resembles fine breadcrumbs. Stir in the sugar and almonds. Add the water and mix to a dough. Lightly knead on a floured surface for a few seconds. Wrap in clear film and chill for 30 minutes.

2 Preheat the oven to 200°C/400°F/ Gas 6. Roll out the pastry on a lightly floured surface to a 25cm/10in circle and use it to line the base and sides of a 20cm/8in tart tin. Trim the edges of the pastry with a sharp knife.

3 Prick with a fork, cover with oiled foil and bake for 6 minutes. Remove the foil and bake for 6 more minutes. Allow to cool and reduce the temperature to 150°C/300°F/Gas 2.

4 For the filling, cream the butter, sugar and vanilla essence together. Beat in one egg, then stir in the flour. Beat the cheese until soft, then gradually mix in the remaining eggs. Blend this into the butter mixture. Stir in the lemon rind, juice and raisins.

5 Pour the filling over the pastry base. Bake in the oven for 1½ hours, until firm. Turn off the oven, leave the door ajar and allow to cool before removing. Dust with icing sugar.

Polish Pancakes

Fluffy pancakes are filled with a cheese and sultana mixture.

INGREDIENTS

Makes 6
115g/4oz/1 cup plain flour
pinch of salt
pinch of grated nutmeg, plus extra
    for dusting
1 egg, separated
200ml/7fl oz/scant 1 cup milk
30ml/2 tbsp sunflower oil
25g/1oz/2 tbsp butter
lemon slices, to garnish

For the filling
225g/8oz/1 cup curd cheese
15ml/1 tbsp caster sugar
5ml/1 tsp vanilla essence
50g/2oz/scant ½ cup sultanas

1 Sift the flour, salt and nutmeg together in a large bowl. Make a well in the centre. Add the yolk and half of the milk. Beat until smooth, then gradually beat in the remaining milk.

2 Whisk the egg white in a bowl until stiff. Fold into the batter.

3 Heat 5ml/1 tsp sunflower oil and a little of the butter in an 18cm/7in frying pan. Pour in enough of the batter to cover the base.

4 Cook for 2 minutes, until golden brown, then turn over and cook for a further 2 minutes.

5 Make 5 more pancakes in the same way, using more oil and butter as necessary. Stack up the pancakes and keep them warm.

6 To make the filling, put the curd cheese, sugar and vanilla essence in a bowl and beat together. Mix in the sultanas. Divide among the pancakes, fold them up and dust with grated nutmeg. Garnish with lemon slices.

Apricot Treat

Fresh fruit was once scarce in Poland during winter, so dried fruits were often used. This rich apricot and almond dessert, a favourite in Poland, resembles the sweetmeats more common to the Balkan regions.

INGREDIENTS

Serves 6
225g/8oz/1 cup ready-to-eat
   dried apricots, chopped
45ml/3 tbsp water
50g/2oz/¼ cup caster sugar
50g/2oz/½ cup chopped almonds
50g/2oz/⅓ cup chopped candied
   orange peel
icing sugar, for dusting
whipped cream, to serve
ground cinnamon, to decorate

1 Put the apricots and water in a heavy-based pan. Cover and simmer, stirring, for about 20 minutes, until a thick paste forms.

2 Stir in the caster sugar and simmer, stirring, for a further 10 minutes until quite dry. Remove from the heat and stir in the almonds and chopped orange peel.

3 Using a knife, shape into a "sausage", about 5cm/2in thick, on a piece of greaseproof paper dusted with icing sugar.

4 Leave to dry in a cool place for at least 3 hours. Cut into slices and serve with whipped cream, sprinkled with a little cinnamon.

Dried Fruit Compote

Fruit grows in abundance in orchards throughout the Ukraine and dried fruits are used all year round. *Uzvar* is served on Christmas Eve and also at feasts at which the dead are honoured. This easy and delicious dessert is also made in Russia.

INGREDIENTS

Serves 6
350g/12oz/2 cups mixed dried fruits,
   such as apples, pears, prunes, peaches
   or apricots
1 cinnamon stick
300ml/½ pint/1¼ cups cider or water
65g/2½oz/½ cup raisins
30ml/2 tbsp clear honey
juice of ½ lemon
mint leaves, to decorate

1 Put the mixed dried fruit in a large pan with the cinnamon and cider or water. Heat gently until almost boiling, then cover the pan, lower the heat and cook gently for 12–15 minutes, to soften the fruit.

--- COOK'S TIP ---

This compote will keep refrigerated for up to a week.

2 Remove the pan from the heat and stir in the raisins and honey. Cover the pan and leave to cool. Remove the cinnamon stick and then stir in the lemon juice.

3 Transfer the compote to a serving bowl, cover with clear film and keep refrigerated until needed. Allow the fruit compote to come to room temperature before serving, decorated with a few mint leaves.

Plum and Almond Tart

Plums and almonds have a natural affinity, and this Russian tart with its simple pastry case is a great way to serve them. Serve with home-made custard.

INGREDIENTS

Serves 6
175g/6oz/1½ cups plain flour
115g/4oz/8 tbsp butter, chilled
60ml/4 tbsp soured cream

For the topping
50g/2oz/4 tbsp butter, softened
50g/2oz/¼ cup caster sugar, plus
    30ml/2 tbsp for sprinkling
2 eggs, beaten
115g/4oz/1 cup ground almonds
about 6 plums, quartered and stoned
115g/4oz/scant ½ cup plum jam
60ml/4 tbsp flaked almonds

1 Sift the flour into a mixing bowl. Dice the butter and rub in until the mixture resembles fine breadcrumbs. Stir in the soured cream to make a soft dough. Wrap in clear film and chill for at least 30 minutes.

COOK'S TIP

Apricots can be used instead of plums, as an alternative, if liked.

2 For the topping, cream the butter and sugar until light. Add the eggs, alternating with the ground almonds.

3 Preheat the oven to 220°C/425°F/ Gas 7. Roll out the pastry on a lightly floured surface to a 30cm/12in round, then transfer to a large baking sheet. Prick all over.

4 Spread the almond mixture over the pastry, leaving a border of about 4cm/1½in. Arrange the plums on top. Sprinkle with the 30ml/2 tbsp caster sugar. Turn in the border.

5 Bake the tart for 35–40 minutes, or until browned. Warm the plum jam in a small pan, press through a sieve and brush over the tart to glaze. Sprinkle flaked almonds on top to decorate.

VARIATION

The recipe could be used to make 4 individual tarts, like the one shown here. Thickly slice the plums instead of cutting them into quarters. Finish the tarts as above with the jam glaze and flaked almonds.

Lepeshki

With characteristic Russian preference for all things sour, these biscuits are shortened with soured cream instead of butter.

INGREDIENTS

Makes 24

225g/8oz/2 cups self-raising flour
pinch of salt
90g/3½oz/½ cup caster sugar
1 egg, separated
120ml/4fl oz/½ cup soured cream
2.5ml/½ tsp each vanilla and
   almond essence
15ml/1 tbsp milk
50g/2oz/½ cup flaked almonds

1 Preheat the oven to 200°C/400°F/ Gas 6. Sift the flour, salt and sugar into a mixing bowl and make a well in the centre.

2 Reserve 10ml/2 tsp of the egg white. Mix the remainder with the egg yolk, soured cream, vanilla and almond essences and milk. Add to the dry ingredients and mix to form a soft dough.

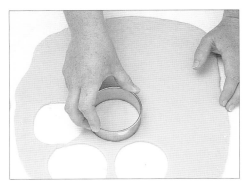

3 Roll out the dough on a lightly floured surface until about 8mm/⅓in thick, then stamp out rounds with a 7.5cm/3in cutter.

4 Transfer the circles to lightly oiled baking sheets. Brush with the reserved egg white and sprinkle with the flaked almonds.

5 Bake for 10 minutes, until light golden brown. Transfer to a wire rack and allow to cool. Store the biscuits in an airtight container.

Babka

A typical Polish Easter menu is a grand affair and may include roast sucking pig, brightly coloured eggs and *Babka* – the word means "Grandmother". The cake was so named because it is made with gentleness and loving care.

INGREDIENTS

Serves 8
350g/12oz/3 cups plain flour
2.5ml/¹/₂ tsp salt
25g/1oz/2 tbsp caster sugar
5ml/1 tsp easy-blend dried yeast
115g/4oz/8 tbsp butter, softened
150ml/¹/₄ pint/²/₃ cup warm milk
4 egg yolks
115g/4oz/scant 1 cup sultanas
finely grated rind of 1 orange
60ml/4 tbsp clear honey, warmed
butter, to serve

1 Sift the flour, salt and sugar into a large bowl. Stir in the yeast, then make a well in the centre.

2 Add the butter, milk, egg yolks, dried fruit and orange rind. Mix to a dough. Turn out on a lightly floured surface and knead for 10 minutes, until smooth and elastic.

3 Put the dough in a well-greased 1.25kg/2¹/₂lb fluted cake tin. Cover with oiled clear film and leave in a warm place to rise for 1 hour, or until doubled in size.

4 Preheat the oven to 190°C/375°F/ Gas 5. Bake for 45–50 minutes, or until firm and a skewer inserted into the middle comes out clean.

5 Allow the cake to cool in the tin for 5 minutes. Turn out on to a wire rack and brush all over with the warmed honey. When cold, slice thickly and serve with butter.

Christmas Cookies

These spiced biscuits may be used as edible decorations: thread them with coloured ribbon and hang on the branches of the Christmas tree, as is traditionally done in the Ukraine.

INGREDIENTS

Makes 30
50g/2oz/4 tbsp butter
15ml/1 tbsp golden syrup or
  clear honey
50g/2oz/¹/₄ cup soft light brown sugar
225g/8oz/2 cups plain flour
10ml/2 tsp ground cinnamon
5ml/1 tsp ground ginger
1.5ml/¹/₄ tsp grated nutmeg
2.5ml/¹/₂ tsp bicarbonate of soda
45ml/3 tbsp milk
1 egg yolk
30ml/2 tbsp sugar crystals

1 Preheat the oven to 180°C/350°F/ Gas 4. Line 2 baking sheets with baking parchment. Melt the butter, syrup or honey and brown sugar in a pan. Leave to cool for 5 minutes.

2 Sift the flour, cinnamon, ginger, nutmeg and bicarbonate of soda into a bowl. Make a well in the centre. Pour in the melted butter mixture, milk and egg yolk. Mix to a soft dough.

3 Knead until smooth, then roll out between 2 sheets of baking parchment until 5mm/¹/₄in thick. Stamp out rounds using biscuit cutters.

--- COOK'S TIP ---

Roll out the dough while it is still warm, since it becomes hard and brittle as it cools.

4 Place on the baking sheets. Make a hole in each with a skewer if you wish to hang them up later. Sprinkle with coloured sugar crystals. Bake for 10 minutes, until a slightly darker shade. Cool slightly, then transfer to a wire rack and leave to cool completely.

Sour Rye Bread

Traditionally, the "starter" would be a little dough left over from a previous bread-making session, but it's simple to make your own. The starter gives this bread its delicious, slightly sour taste.

INGREDIENTS

Makes 2 loaves
450g/1lb/4 cups rye flour, plus extra
    for dusting (optional)
450g/1lb/4 cups strong white flour
15ml/1 tbsp salt
7g/¼ oz sachet easy-blend
    dried yeast
25g/1oz/2 tbsp butter, softened
600ml/1 pint/2½ cups warm water
15ml/1 tbsp caraway seeds or
    buckwheat, for sprinkling (optional)

For the sourdough starter
60ml/4 tbsp rye flour
45ml/3 tbsp warm milk

1 For the starter, mix the rye flour and milk together in a small bowl. Cover with clear film and leave in a warm place for 1–2 days, or until it smells pleasantly sour.

2 To make the loaves, sift together the flour and salt into a large bowl. Next stir in the yeast. Make a well in the centre and add the butter, water and sourdough starter already prepared. With a wooden spoon mix well until you have a soft dough.

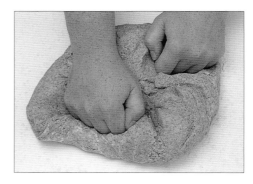

3 Turn out the dough on to a lightly floured surface and knead for 10 minutes, until smooth and elastic. Put in a clean bowl, cover with clear film and leave in a warm place to rise for 1 hour, or until doubled in size.

4 Knead for 1 minute, then divide the dough in half. Shape each piece into a round 15cm/6in across. Transfer to 2 greased baking sheets. Cover with oiled clear film and leave to rise for 30 minutes.

5 Preheat the oven to 200°C/400°F/ Gas 6. Brush the loaves with water, then sprinkle with caraway seeds or buckwheat, or dust with rye flour.

6 Bake for 35–40 minutes, or until the loaves are browned and sound hollow when tapped on the bottom. Cool on a wire rack.

COOK'S TIP

Sour rye bread keeps fresh for up to a week. This recipe can also be made without yeast, but it will be much denser.

Poppy Seed Roll

This sweet yeast bake with its spiral filling of dried fruits and poppy seeds is a wonderful example of traditional Polish cooking and is a firm favourite. The seeds have a gritty texture and keep the cake moist.

INGREDIENTS

Serves 12
450g/1lb/4 cups plain flour
pinch of salt
30ml/2 tbsp caster sugar
10ml/2 tsp easy-blend dried yeast
175ml/6fl oz/³/₄ cup milk
finely grated rind of 1 lemon
50g/2oz/4 tbsp butter

For the filling and glaze
50g/2oz/4 tbsp butter
115g/4oz/²/₃ cup poppy seeds
50ml/2fl oz/¹/₄ cup set honey
65g/2¹/₂ oz/¹/₂ cup raisins
65g/2¹/₂ oz/scant ¹/₂ cup finely
    chopped candied orange peel
50g/2oz/¹/₂ cup ground almonds
1 egg yolk
50g/2oz/¹/₄ cup caster sugar
15ml/1 tbsp milk
60ml/4 tbsp apricot jam
15ml/1 tbsp lemon juice
15ml/1 tbsp rum or brandy
25g/1oz/¹/₄ cup toasted
    flaked almonds

1 Sift the flour, salt and sugar into a bowl. Stir in the easy-blend dried yeast. Make a well in the centre.

2 Heat the milk and lemon rind in a pan with the butter, until melted. Cool a little, then add to the dry ingredients and mix to a dough.

3 Knead the dough on a lightly floured surface for 10 minutes, until smooth and elastic. Put in a clean bowl, cover and leave in a warm place to rise for 45–50 minutes, or until doubled in size.

4 For the filling, melt the butter in a pan. Reserve 15ml/1 tbsp of poppy seeds, then process the rest and add to the pan with the honey, raisins and peel. Cook gently for 5 minutes. Stir in the almonds; leave to cool.

5 Whisk the egg yolk and sugar together in a bowl until pale, then fold into the poppy seed mixture. Roll out the dough on a lightly floured surface to a rectangle 30 × 35cm/ 12 × 14in. Spread the filling to within 2.5cm/1in of the edges.

6 Roll both ends towards the centre. Cover with oiled clear film and leave to rise for 30 minutes. Preheat the oven to 190°C/375°F/Gas 5.

7 Brush with the milk, then sprinkle with the reserved poppy seeds. Bake for 30 minutes, until golden brown.

8 Heat the jam and lemon juice gently until bubbling. Sieve, then stir in the rum or brandy. Brush over the roll while still warm and scatter the almonds on top.

GERMANY, AUSTRIA, HUNGARY AND THE CZECH REPUBLIC

Drawing on influences from Russia to France and Turkey, the cooking of this area is famous for its filling stews and dumplings, distinctive use of ingredients such as sauerkraut and paprika, and excellence in cake and pastry making.

INTRODUCTION

The Central European countries of Germany, Austria, Hungary, the Czech Republic and Slovakia comprise a geographical region that extends southwards from the cold shores of the North and Baltic Seas to the warmer climes of the Balkan countries. The foods characteristic of this area thus reflect a wide range of influences, though is dominated by a robust style that is famous world-wide.

CULINARY IDENTITY

On the everyday level of eating and drinking, national tastes within Central Europe have tended to remain simple and relatively distinct. The wide availability of many typical ingredients, however, such as caraway seeds, cucumbers, dill, mustard, soured cream and cabbage, has naturally resulted in an overlap of cooking styles, and sometimes recipes of neighbouring countries may vary only slightly in ingredients or method.

Czech cooking, for example, is solid and satisfying and bland in flavour except for the use of marjoram. Pale rye bread is preferred, as are salads of potato and other cooked vegetables, often dressed with mayonnaise. Potatoes are also fried with bacon or simmered with sausage to make quickly prepared supper dishes. Versatile use is made of other root crops such as kohlrabi and celeriac. The best loved of all Czech dishes however, has to be the dumpling. Made of flour, semolina or potato, in all shapes and sizes, these are served in savoury soups and stews as well as dessert dishes.

In contrast with such mild flavours and hefty textures, Hungarian cooking can be quite fiery and is rich in Mediterranean-style vegetables. The sour flavours and pickles that are so characteristic of the rest of Eastern Europe are less often seen in Hungarian cooking. The abundance of wheat ensures plenty of robust white bread, in place of darker breads, and more use of home-made pasta.

HUNGARIAN FINESSE

In the best of Hungarian cooking, as in some German cuisine, the use of red and white wine in meat and fish dishes has produced a greater complexity and subtlety than in other Central European cuisines, establishing a dividing line between good Hungarian cooking and the more usual country-style fare of the region. Hungarian chefs also have different ways of cooking meat and fish with paprika, according to whether or not the finished dish is

Left: The following collection of recipes concentrates on the Central European countries, where hearty peasant traditions sit alongside the opulence of dishes that flourished during the period of the great Austro-Hungarian Hapsburg Empire.

Right: Fresh produce available in the markets ranges from root vegetables characteristic of northern Europe to tomatoes, courgettes and peppers, more typical of the warmer southern cuisines.

dry or whether it contains cream. Goulash itself is always a dish with plenty of sauce.

It appears that the development of such fine Hungarian cuisine and the adoption of a wide variety of ingredients, including tomatoes, onions and peppers, was a consequence of an important royal marriage in the 15th century. In 1475 King Matthias married the daughter of the King of Naples, who imported new ingredients and chefs to make life beyond Italy's borders bearable. From these early refinements, Hungarian cuisine has rarely looked back.

MEAT DISHES

A key ingredient of this region's cooking is pork. Although the world-famous Austrian schnitzel is usually made with veal, across Germany and the other Central European countries pork is more commonly eaten, either as fried breadcrumbed steaks or cooked with peppers. In the Czech Republic, it is also often served wrapped around an egg, ham and cheese filling. It is also often stewed as a variation on the classic Hungarian goulash.

Cured pork, or bacon, provides another important ingredient in Central European cooking, valued for its unique pervasive flavour. Czech and Hungarian cooks, for instance, use bacon fat to achieve the distinctive tastes of many soups and otherwise meat-free fare, including dishes of long-simmered red cabbage.

Pork is also the major ingredient of the region's sausages. Czech sausages and Hungarian salami are famous worldwide, and every German region has its distinctive *wurst*, or sausage.

Beef perhaps rivals pork in popularity only in those parts of Central Eastern Europe where the best cattle are raised. One such place is the central Hungarian plain, or *puszta*, the original home of goulash, which is named after the *gulyás* (cowherds) who invented the prototype dish. While today's tempting recipes for this classic dish make use of paprika, caraway, green peppers and tomatoes, the cowherds of past centuries simply added water to meat they had previously cooked with onions then dried in the sun.

Although it has no such romantic history, German beef cookery is also excellent: for instance, recipes for *sauerbraten*, beef marinated in vinegar, sugar and seasonings then braised, serve simply to show off high-quality beef at its best.

JEWISH HERITAGE

Much of Central and Eastern European cuisine is known to the West in the guise of Jewish cooking, dating from the time when many Jewish communities inhabited this part of Europe. Czech and traditional Jewish cooking, for instance, share a taste for goose and beef as well as for carp served in sweetish sauces. Jewish *gefilte fisch*, carp stuffed with pike, uses two of the classic fish of the region. Pancakes, beans and fried cakes of grated raw potato figure in both cuisines. The Jewish Sabbath dish of *cholent*, bean and barley stew, is simply a kosher variation of the pork versions of the dish found everywhere in Central Europe. By the same token, Jewish recipes for red cabbage dispense with bacon.

CAKES AND SWEET PASTRIES

The fine tradition of cakes and sweet pastries common to southern Germany, Austria and Hungary owes much to the bread and pastry cooks of 18th-century Vienna, who in turn were inspired by a mixture of French and Turkish influences. German, Austro-Hungarian and Jewish cakemakers of the past two and a half centuries have together created the greatest torten and strudels in the world, and the most civilized surroundings in which to eat them while drinking coffee.

While the range of cakes available is great, a good plain cake which straddles all borders is the *gugelhupf* or *kugelhupf*. This is leavened with yeast and traditionally baked in a Turk's head mould.

INGREDIENTS

VEGETABLES

Fresh red and green peppers of the large capsicum variety, tomatoes and courgettes, parsley and dill are among the abundant vegetables and fresh herbs you would expect to see in a Hungarian market. In addition to large onions for cooking, spring onions are used in salads and to garnish soups. The more unusual root crops in Germany and the Czech lands include kohlrabi, a relative of the cabbage family, and celeriac, a large knobby root vegetable, which can be used in soups or salads.

MEAT AND POULTRY

Fresh pork is most popular, with goose cooked for special occasions. Central European food is most famous, however, for its smoked and unsmoked pork sausage and bacon. Bacon teams particularly well with cabbage and caraway, and

bacon fat is often used to enhance the flavour of soups and stews. As for sausages, from Germany through the Czech Republic to Slovakia and Hungary, these are eternally popular street food, eaten simply with mustard and a roll, and they double as quick meals in pubs and restaurants. The number of varieties available from shops and delicatessens, from the frankfurter style to juicy fat specimens, can easily overwhelm the uninitiated. The range of salami-style sausage, which in German is called *wurst*, is equally wide and delicious.

GRAINS

Central Europe is the home of *mehlspeisen*, dishes of noodles or dumplings, which can be either sweet or savoury and take the place of a main meal. Dumplings are made of flour and semolina and sometimes include potato. Good wholemeal white flour is essential for fine baking, and excellent white bread is produced alongside traditional pale rye bread.

HERBS, SPICES AND OTHER FLAVOURINGS

Paprika was introduced to daily Hungarian cooking by the Turks some time before the 17th century, but it took a long time before the upper classes adopted the habit. To make paprika powder, the fleshy parts of peppers are dried and powdered, with a proportion of their seeds. The result is graded according to piquancy, fineness and colour, with the colours varying from bright red to yellowish brown. "Sweet noble" paprika is darker and more piquant than the

Above left: capsicum, tomatoes, celeriac, onions and kohlrabi.

Above right: assorted German breads, including sour dough, pumperknickel, rye and poppy seed.

Right, clockwise from front left: smoked loin, Hungarian guylai, *pork medallion steaks, boned shoulder, pork ribs,* bauernbratwurst, regensburgers *and* frankfurters.

Above, anticlockwise from left: apples, plums, cherries, hazelnuts and almonds

Left, from left to right: dried chillies, paprika and fresh and bottled chillies

duller, lighter, half-sweet paprika, which can give a good colour to a dish without making it unbearably hot. Many Hungarian dishes are begun by lightly frying an onion and sprinkling some paprika powder over it.

Caraway seed, which has a cooling and digestive effect, is widely used in cabbage dishes and with pork. The flowery, pungent taste of fresh marjoram, which retains its flavour uniquely well among herbs when dried, is a year-round favourite with Czech cooks. Mustard of a mild European variety is the essential accompaniment to the boiled sausages of Central East Europe.

In baking, honey, poppy seeds and cake spices, such as cinnamon, cloves and cardamom, are used to flavour traditional sweet biscuits and breads, including gingerbread and plaited buns.

Right, clockwise from left: fresh marjoram; plain, dill and wholegrain mustards; cardamom; cinnamon sticks; poppy seeds; caraway seeds and allspice.

FRUIT

The plums, apricots and cherries of Central Europe make outstanding jams and pie fillings. Apples are widely used and are delicious with braised red cabbage. Germany is one of the largest apple-growing countries in the world, and there is seemingly no limit to the guises in which apples can appear, from strudels and pancakes to cakes.

DAIRY PRODUCTS

Hungarian *lipto* cheese is a speciality ewe's milk cheese, and is the chief ingredient in *liptauer,* a spread made with butter, paprika, caraway and onion. Curd cheese is used in savoury and sweet cooking.

DRINKS

Czech beer from Plsen is arguably the finest in the world. Whatever the country of origin, German lager-style beer is enjoyed throughout Central Eastern Europe and is sometimes used in cooking.

Modest white table wines are produced in Moravia and Slovakia, but the best wine comes from Hungary, from around Lake Balaton and a little further north in the prized Badacsonyi region, and also in the south in Villany, close to Croatia and Serbia. Hungary is also famous for its very sweet dessert wine called *tokai,* produced in a small area in the north of the country, straddling the border with Slovakia. It may be drunk at both the beginning and end of a meal, or added to consommé.

Each Central European country has its favourite brandy or what the Germans call schnapps. One well-known example is the Hungarian *palinka,* made out of apricots. *Slivowicz,* made from plums, is common everywhere. A Czech speciality is a sweetish herbal liqueur called *bekerovka.*

SOUPS AND STARTERS

Soups are a favourite in this area, served either as a main meal or as a starter.
Hearty soups range from creamy dishes such as Czech Cauliflower Soup
accompanied by light dumplings, to the famous fruit soups of Hungary and
chunky soups of Germany, such as Lentil Soup containing sliced frankfurter.
Many central European starters consist of sour vegetables, cold meats, fish and
cheese. Served hot or cold, tasty starters such as Potato Pancakes and
Herby Liver Pâté Pie are ideal as snacks to serve with drinks.

Cream of Spinach Soup

Rich and smooth, Hungarian creamed soups are made with double or soured cream and sometimes egg yolk, too.

INGREDIENTS

Serves 4

500g/1¼lb fresh young spinach, well washed
1.2 litres/2 pints/5 cups salted water
2 onions, very finely chopped or minced
25g/1oz/2 tbsp butter
45ml/3 tbsp plain flour
250ml/8fl oz/1 cup double cream
salt and freshly ground black pepper
2 hard-boiled eggs, sliced, and 2 grilled rindless bacon rashers, crumbled, to garnish

1 Remove and discard any coarse stems from the spinach leaves. Bring the salted water to the boil in a large pan. Add the spinach and cook for 5–6 minutes. Strain the spinach and reserve the liquid.

2 Blend the spinach in a food processor or blender to a purée.

3 Fry the chopped or minced onions in the butter in a large pan until pale golden brown. Remove from the heat and sprinkle in the flour. Return to the heat and cook for a further 1–2 minutes to cook the flour.

4 Stir in the reserved spinach liquid and, once it is all incorporated into the soup, bring it back to the boil.

5 Cook until thick then stir in the spinach purée and double cream. Reheat and adjust the seasoning. Serve the soup in bowls garnished with extra pepper, the sliced eggs and sprinkled with the crumbled bacon pieces.

Lentil Soup

This is a wonderfully hearty German *Linsensuppe*, but a lighter version can be made by omitting the frankfurters, if preferred.

INGREDIENTS

Serves 6

225g/8oz/1 cup brown lentils
15ml/1 tbsp sunflower oil
1 onion, finely chopped
1 leek, finely chopped
1 carrot, finely diced
2 celery sticks, chopped
115g/4oz piece of lean bacon
2 bay leaves
1.5 litres/2½ pints/6¼ cups water
30ml/2 tbsp chopped fresh parsley,
    plus extra to garnish
225g/8oz frankfurter, sliced
salt and freshly ground black pepper

1 Rinse the lentils thoroughly under cold running water.

2 Heat the oil in a large pan and gently fry the onion for 5 minutes, until soft. Add the leek, carrot, celery, bacon and bay leaves.

3 Add the lentils. Pour in the water, then slowly bring to the boil. Skim the surface then simmer, half-covered, for 45–50 minutes, or until the lentils are soft.

4 Remove the piece of bacon from the soup and cut into small cubes. Trim off any excess fat.

5 Return to the soup with the parsley and sliced frankfurter, and season with salt and pepper. Simmer for 2–3 minutes, remove the bay leaves, and serve garnished with the parsley.

COOK'S TIP

Unlike most pulses, brown lentils do not need to be soaked before cooking.

Cauliflower Soup

This puréed soup has the smooth texture typical of Czech soups.

INGREDIENTS

Serves 6–8

1 large cauliflower, cut into florets
1.5 litres/2½ pints/6¼ cups water
  or chicken stock
40g/1½ oz/3 tbsp butter
40g/1½ oz/⅓ cup plain flour
generous pinch of nutmeg or mace
2 egg yolks
300ml/½ pint/1¼ cups whipping cream
flat leaf parsley, to garnish
crusty bread, to serve

For the dumplings

75g/3oz/1½ cups white breadcrumbs
10g/¼ oz/½ tbsp butter, softened
1 egg, beaten
10ml/2 tsp chopped fresh parsley
a little milk, to bind
salt and freshly ground black pepper

1 Cook the cauliflower in the water or chicken stock for 12 minutes or until just tender. Remove and reserve the cooking liquid and a few florets of the cauliflower.

2 Make a sauce by melting the butter in a small pan. Add the flour and cook for 1–2 minutes, before adding about 150ml/¼ pint/⅔ cup of the reserved cauliflower cooking liquid and stirring well. Remove from the heat.

3 Purée the cooked cauliflower in a food processor or blender until smooth. Beat the nutmeg or mace and egg yolks into the cauliflower, then add to the pan of sauce.

4 Add enough cauliflower liquid to make up to 1.2 litres/2 pints/5 cups. Reheat the soup.

5 Make up the dumplings by mixing all the ingredients together. Roll into firm small balls.

6 Poach the dumplings gently in the soup for 3–5 minutes before adding the whipping cream. Garnish with sprigs of flat leaf parsley and the reserved cauliflower and serve with crusty bread.

Fish Soup with Dumplings

This Czech soup takes little time to make compared with a meat-based one. Use a variety of whatever fish is available, such as perch, catfish, cod, snapper or carp. The basis of the dumplings is the same whether you use semolina or flour.

INGREDIENTS

Serves 4–8

3 rindless bacon rashers, diced
675g/1½lb assorted fresh fish, skinned, boned and diced
15ml/1 tbsp paprika, plus extra to garnish
1.5 litres/2½ pints/6¼ cups fish stock or water
3 firm tomatoes, peeled and chopped
4 waxy potatoes, peeled and grated
5–10ml/1–2 tsp chopped fresh marjoram, plus extra to garnish

For the dumplings

75g/3oz/½ cup semolina or flour
1 egg, beaten
45ml/3 tbsp milk or water
generous pinch of salt
15ml/1 tbsp chopped fresh parsley

1 Dry fry the diced bacon in a large pan until pale golden brown, then add the pieces of assorted fish. Fry for 1–2 minutes, taking care not to break up the pieces of fish.

2 Sprinkle in the paprika, pour in the fish stock or water, bring to the boil and simmer for 10 minutes.

3 Stir the tomatoes, grated potato and marjoram into the pan. Cook for 10 minutes, stirring occasionally.

4 Meanwhile, make the dumplings by mixing all the ingredients together, then leave to stand, covered with clear film, for 5–10 minutes.

5 Drop spoonfuls into the soup and cook for 10 minutes. Serve hot, with a little marjoram and paprika.

Hungarian Sour Cherry Soup

Particularly popular in summer, this fruit soup is typical of Hungarian cooking. The recipe makes good use of the plump, sour cherries available locally. Fruit soups are thickened with flour, and a touch of salt is added to help bring out the flavour of this cold soup.

INGREDIENTS

Serves 4
15ml/1 tbsp plain flour
120ml/4fl oz/½ cup soured cream
generous pinch of salt
5ml/1 tsp caster sugar
225g/8oz/1½ cups fresh sour or
    morello cherries, stoned
900ml/1½ pints/3¾ cups water
50g/2oz/¼ cup sugar

1 Blend the flour with the soured cream; add the salt and caster sugar.

2 Cook the cherries in the water, with the sugar. Gently poach for about 10 minutes.

— COOK'S TIP —

The soup is best made with fresh sour or cooking cherries such as morello; the flavour is simply not the same when canned, frozen or bottled cherries are used.

3 Remove from the heat and set aside 30ml/2 tbsp of the cooking liquid as a garnish. Stir another 30ml/2 tbsp of the cherry liquid into the flour and soured cream mixture then pour this on to the cherries.

4 Return to the heat. Bring to the boil then simmer for 5–6 minutes.

5 Remove from the heat, cover with clear film and leave to cool. Add extra salt if necessary. Serve with a little cooking liquid swirled in.

Czech Pork Soup

Originally, this soup would have been made from half or quarter of a pig's head, but these days a shoulder of pork is a little easier to procure and just as tasty.

INGREDIENTS

Serves 4–6
350g/12oz lean shoulder of pork or
    tenderloin, cut into 1cm/½in cubes
1 large onion, finely sliced
115g/4oz/⅔ cup carrots, finely diced
3 garlic cloves, crushed
1.5 litres/2½ pints/6¼ cups water or
    pork stock
10ml/2 tsp chopped fresh marjoram
60–90ml/4–6 tbsp freshly cooked
    pearl barley or long grain rice
salt and freshly ground black pepper

1 Put the pork cubes, onion, carrot and garlic in a large pan. Pour in the water or stock.

— COOK'S TIP —

For a more substantial soup, double the quantity of barley or rice.

2 Simmer for 1–1½ hours, or until the meat is just tender.

3 Skim, if necessary, before adding the marjoram. Season to taste. Simmer for a further 5–10 minutes.

4 Place the barley or rice in serving bowls then ladle over the soup.

Stuffed Mushrooms with Spinach

The large, flat, wild or cultivated mushrooms are excellent in this recipe, but use fresh ceps instead for perfection.

INGREDIENTS

Serves 6
12 large flat mushrooms
450g/1lb small young spinach leaves, well washed
3 rindless bacon rashers, cut into 5mm/¼in dice
1 onion, finely chopped
2 egg yolks, beaten
40g/1½oz/¾ cup fresh breadcrumbs
5ml/1 tsp chopped fresh marjoram
45ml/3 tbsp olive or vegetable oil
115g/4oz/1 cup feta cheese, crumbled
salt and freshly ground black pepper

1 Peel the mushrooms only if necessary. Remove the stalks and chop them finely.

2 Blanch the spinach by dropping into a pan of boiling water for 1–2 minutes, then plunge into cold water. Squeeze the spinach in kitchen paper, drying it thoroughly to prevent the filling being watery, then chop.

3 Dry fry the bacon rashers and chopped onion together in a pan until golden brown, then add the mushroom stalks. Remove from the heat. Stir in the spinach, egg yolks, breadcrumbs and marjoram and season to taste.

4 Place the mushrooms on a baking sheet and brush with a little oil.

5 Place heaped tablespoons of the spinach mixture on to the mushroom caps. Sprinkle over the cheese and cook the mushrooms under a preheated grill for about 10 minutes, or until golden brown.

Potato Pancakes

These little snacks are popular
street food in the Czech
Republic, and they are available
at roadside stalls and cafés.
Quick and easy to make, they
are a tasty adaptation of the
classic flour-based pancake.

INGREDIENTS

Serves 6–8
6 large waxy potatoes, peeled
2 eggs, beaten
1–2 garlic cloves, crushed
115g/4oz/1 cup plain flour
5ml/1 tsp chopped fresh marjoram
50g/2oz/4 tbsp butter
60ml/4 tbsp oil
salt and freshly ground black pepper
soured cream, chopped fresh parsley
   and a tomato salad, to serve

1 Grate the potatoes and squeeze
thoroughly dry, using a dish towel.

2 Put the potatoes in a bowl with the
eggs, garlic, flour, marjoram and
seasoning and mix well.

3 Heat half the butter and oil
together in a large frying pan then
add large spoonfuls of the potato
mixture to form rounds. Carefully
flatten the "pancakes" well with the
back of a dampened spoon.

— COOK'S TIP —

Put potatoes in water with a few drops of
lemon, to prevent them turning brown.

4 Fry the pancakes until crisp and
golden brown then turn over and
cook on the other side. Drain on
kitchen paper and keep warm while
cooking the rest of the pancakes,
adding the remaining butter and oil to
the frying pan as necessary.

5 Serve the pancakes topped with
soured cream, sprinkled with
parsley, and accompanied by a fresh,
juicy tomato salad.

Herby Liver Pâté Pie

A delicious luncheon dish with a glass of Plsen beer.

INGREDIENTS

Serves 10
675g/1½lb minced pork
350g/12oz pork liver
350g/12oz/2 cups cooked ham, diced
1 small onion, finely chopped
30ml/2 tbsp chopped fresh parsley
5ml/1 tsp German mustard
30ml/2 tbsp Kirsch
5ml/1 tsp salt
beaten egg, for sealing and glazing
25g/1oz sachet aspic jelly
250ml/8fl oz/1 cup boiling water
freshly ground black pepper
bread and dill pickles, to serve

For the pastry
450g/1lb/4 cups plain flour
pinch of salt
275g/10oz/1¼ cups butter
2 eggs
1 egg yolk
30ml/2 tbsp water

1 Preheat the oven to 200°C/400°F/ Gas 6. To make the pastry, sift the flour and salt and rub in the butter. Beat the eggs, egg yolk and water, add to the dry ingredients and mix.

2 Knead the dough briefly until smooth. Roll out two-thirds on a lightly floured surface and use to line a 10 × 25cm/4 × 10in hinged loaf tin. Trim any excess dough.

3 Process half the pork and the liver until fairly smooth. Stir in the remaining minced pork, ham, onion, parsley, mustard, Kirsch and seasoning.

4 Spoon the filling into the tin, smoothing it down and levelling the surface.

5 Roll out the remaining pastry on the lightly floured surface and use it to top the pie, sealing the edges with some of the beaten egg. Decorate with the pastry trimmings and glaze with the remaining beaten egg. Using a fork, make 3 or 4 holes in the top, for the steam to escape.

6 Bake for 40 minutes, then reduce the oven temperature to 180°C/ 350°F/Gas 4 and cook for a further hour. Cover the pastry with foil if the top begins to brown too much. Allow the pie to cool in the tin.

7 Make up the aspic jelly, using the boiling water. Stir to dissolve, then allow to cool.

8 Make a small hole near the edge of the pie with a skewer, then pour in the aspic through a greaseproof paper funnel. Chill for at least 2 hours before serving the pie in slices with mustard, bread and dill pickles.

Vegetable Salad

This salad is a delicious blend of typical Central East European ingredients – soured cream, dill pickle, lemon juice and paprika. It is generally served as a starter alongside cold meats or poultry.

INGREDIENTS

Serves 6

225g/8oz/1½ cups green beans, trimmed
2 carrots, diced
115g/4oz/1 cup fresh or frozen peas
6 egg yolks
15ml/1 tbsp German mustard
30ml/2 tbsp granulated sugar
45ml/3 tbsp freshly squeezed lemon juice
400ml/14fl oz/1⅔ cups soured cream
1 small cooking apple, cored and diced
2–3 celery sticks, diced
1 dill pickle, diced
3 hard-boiled eggs
5ml/1 tsp chopped fresh parsley
30ml/2tbsp fresh breadcrumbs
5ml/1 tsp paprika
salt and freshly ground black pepper

1 Cook the green beans, carrots and peas in a large saucepan of boiling salted water for 5–8 minutes. Drain well then plunge into cold water to refresh. Drain well again.

2 Blend together in a heatproof bowl the egg yolks, mustard, sugar, lemon juice, soured cream and seasoning. Place the bowl containing the mixture over a pan of simmering water, stirring all the time until the sauce starts to thicken.

3 Remove from the heat and stir in the cooked vegetables, apple, celery and dill pickle. Mix well, then cover and chill.

4 Cut the hard-boiled eggs in half lengthways and carefully remove the yolks into a small mixing bowl, keeping the egg whites intact.

5 Blend the cooked egg yolks well with the parsley, breadcrumbs, paprika and a little seasoning. Use the filling to stuff the egg whites. Arrange the chilled vegetables on a serving plate and top with the stuffed eggs.

COOK'S TIP

If German mustard is too strong, replace with either a grainy mustard or chopped fresh tarragon.

MEAT AND POULTRY

Lamb, beef, veal and chicken are all used in Central European cooking, though it is perhaps pork that best exemplifies German and Central European meat cooking. Roasts feature often, as do casseroles and stews, which are often served with dumplings. The sweet-sour flavour so typical across this region is again in evidence with sauces and meat stews containing dill pickles and sauerkraut. In Hungary, however, the presence of paprika, introduced from Turkey, has led to many classic dishes, of which Goulash is just one.

Leg of Lamb with Pickle Sauce

Lamb is generally reserved for special occasions and festivals in Hungary. The sourness of the pickle sauce is an unusual contrast to the rich lamb.

INGREDIENTS

Serves 6–8
1.75kg/4lb lean leg of lamb
30–45ml/2–3 tbsp granular salt
finely grated rind of 1 lemon
50g/2oz/4 tbsp butter
4 rosemary sprigs
handful of flat leaf parsley
extra sprigs of rosemary and flat
  leaf parsley, to garnish
braised red cabbage,
  to serve

For the pickle sauce
8–10 gherkins
25g/1oz/2 tbsp butter
50g/2oz/½ cup flour
250ml/8fl oz/1 cup lamb stock
generous pinch of saffron
30ml/2 tbsp soured cream
5–10ml/1–2 tsp white wine vinegar
salt and freshly ground black pepper

1 Preheat the oven to 180°C/350°F/ Gas 4. Flatten the lamb with a rolling pin, rub with salt; leave for 30 minutes.

2 Mix together the lemon rind and butter. Place the lamb in a roasting tin and spread the lemon butter over.

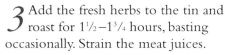

3 Add the fresh herbs to the tin and roast for 1½–1¾ hours, basting occasionally. Strain the meat juices.

4 Meanwhile, make the pickle sauce. Process the gherkins coarsely. Heat the butter in a small pan and cook the gherkins for 5 minutes, stirring occasionally. Remove from the heat. Sprinkle in the flour and stir for a further 2–3 minutes.

5 Slowly pour the stock into the pan and bring to the boil. Stir in the saffron. Allow the sauce to simmer for a further 15 minutes.

6 Off the heat stir in the soured cream, vinegar and the strained meat juices. Season to taste. Garnish with herbs and serve with the sauce and red cabbage.

COOK'S TIP

Let the lamb stand for 10–20 minutes after cooking to allow the fibres in the meat to relax, making it more tender, firmer and easier to carve.

Lamb Goulash with Tomatoes and Peppers

Goulash is a dish that has travelled across Europe from Hungary and is popular in many places such as the Czech Republic and Germany. This Czech recipe is not a true goulash, however, because of the addition of flour. Nevertheless, it has a wonderful infusion of tomatoes, paprika, green peppers and marjoram.

INGREDIENTS

Serves 4–6

30ml/2 tbsp vegetable oil or melted lard (optional)
900g/2lb lean lamb, trimmed and cut into cubes
1 large onion, roughly chopped
2 garlic cloves, crushed
3 green peppers, seeded and diced
30ml/2 tbsp paprika
2 × 397g/14oz cans chopped plum tomatoes
15ml/1tbsp chopped fresh flat leaf parsley
5ml/1 tsp chopped fresh marjoram
30ml/2 tbsp plain flour
60ml/4 tbsp cold water
salt and freshly ground black pepper
green salad, to serve

2 Add the onion and garlic and cook for a further 2 minutes before adding the green peppers and paprika.

1 Heat up the oil or lard, if using, in a frying pan. Dry fry or fry the pieces of lamb for 5–8 minutes, or until browned on all sides. Season well.

3 Pour in the tomatoes and enough water, if needed, to cover the meat in the pan. Stir in the herbs. Bring to the boil, turn down the heat, cover and simmer very gently for 1½ hours, or until the lamb is tender.

4 Blend the flour with the cold water and pour into the stew. Bring back to the boil then reduce the heat to a simmer and cook until the sauce has thickened. Adjust the seasoning and serve the lamb goulash with a crisp green salad.

Loin of Pork with Prune Stuffing

Pork is by far the most popular meat in Germany and appears in many guises. Crushed ginger biscuits are a traditional thickening ingredient and add colour and flavour to a sauce.

INGREDIENTS

Serves 4

1.5kg/3lb cured or smoked loin of pork
75g/3oz/about 18 ready-to-eat prunes, finely chopped
45ml/3 tbsp apple juice or water
75g/3oz/1½ cups day-old ginger biscuit crumbs
3 cardamom pods
15ml/1 tbsp sunflower oil
1 onion, chopped
250ml/8fl oz/1 cup dry red wine
15ml/1 tbsp soft dark brown sugar
salt and freshly ground black pepper
buttery fried stoned prunes and apple and leek slices with steamed green cabbage, to serve

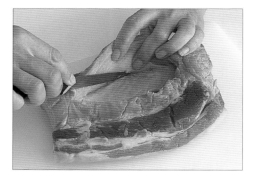

1 Preheat the oven to 230°C/450°F/ Gas 8. Put the pork, fat side down on a board. Make a cut about 3cm/ 1¼in deep along the length to within 1cm/½in of the ends, then make 2 deep cuts to its left and right, to create 2 pockets in the meat.

2 Put the prunes in a bowl. Spoon over the apple juice or water, then add the biscuit crumbs. Remove the cardamom seeds from their pods and crush using a pestle and mortar, or on a board with the end of a rolling pin. Add to the bowl with salt and pepper.

3 Mix the prune stuffing well and use to fill the pockets in the meat.

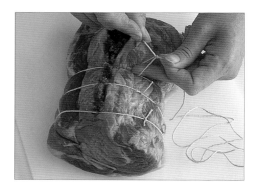

4 Tie the pork joint at regular intervals with string. Heat the oil in a roasting tin set on the hob and brown the joint over a high heat. Remove the meat and set aside.

5 Add the chopped onion to the tin and fry for 10 minutes, until golden. Return the pork to the tin, pour in the wine and add the sugar and seasoning.

6 Roast for 10 minutes, then reduce the oven temperature to 180°C/ 350°F/Gas 4 and roast, uncovered, for a further 1 hour and 50 minutes, or until cooked and golden brown.

7 Remove the joint from the tin and keep warm. Strain the meat juices through a sieve into a pan and simmer for 10 minutes, until slightly reduced. Carve the pork and serve with the sauce separately, accompanied by buttery fried stoned prunes and apple and leek slices, together with steamed green cabbage.

Braised Spicy Spare Ribs

Choose really meaty ribs for this dish and trim off any excess fat before cooking, as the juices are turned into a delicious sauce.

INGREDIENTS

Serves 6
25g/1oz/¼ cup plain flour
5ml/1 tsp salt
5ml/1 tsp ground black pepper
1.5kg/3½lb pork spare ribs, cut into
   individual pieces
30ml/2 tbsp sunflower oil
1 onion, finely chopped
1 garlic clove, crushed
45ml/3 tbsp tomato purée
30ml/2 tbsp chilli sauce
30ml/2 tbsp red wine vinegar
pinch of ground cloves
600ml/1 pint/2½ cups beef stock
15ml/1 tbsp cornflour
flat leaf parsley, to garnish
sauerkraut and crusty bread, to serve

1 Preheat the oven to 180°C/350°F/ Gas 4. Combine the flour, salt and black pepper in a shallow dish. Add the ribs and toss to coat them in flour.

2 Heat the oil in a large frying pan and cook the ribs, turning them until well browned. Transfer them to a roasting tin and sprinkle over the chopped onion.

3 In a bowl, mix together the garlic, tomato purée, chilli sauce, vinegar, cloves and stock. Pour over the ribs, then cover with foil. Roast for 1½ hours, or until tender, removing the foil for the last 30 minutes.

4 Tip the juices from the roasting tin into a small pan. Blend the cornflour in a cup with a little cold water and stir in. Bring the sauce to the boil, stirring, then simmer for 2–3 minutes until thickened.

5 Arrange the ribs on a bed of sauerkraut, then pour over a little sauce. Serve the remaining sauce separately in a warmed jug. Garnish with flat leaf parsley and serve with sauerkraut and crusty bread.

COOK'S TIP

If time allows, first marinate the ribs in sunflower oil mixed with red wine vinegar.

Pork Stew with Sauerkraut

An excellent combination of classic Central European flavours.

INGREDIENTS

Serves 4–6
30ml/2 tbsp vegetable oil or lard
2 onions, finely chopped
2 garlic cloves, crushed
900g/2lb lean pork, cut into 5cm/
   2in cubes
5ml/1 tsp caraway seeds (optional)
15ml/1 tbsp chopped fresh dill
900ml/1½ pints/3¾ cups warm pork
   or vegetable stock
900g/2lb/4 cups sauerkraut, drained
15ml/1 tbsp paprika
salt
dill, to garnish
soured cream, sprinkled with paprika,
   and pickled chillies (optional),
   to serve

1 Heat the oil or lard in a large pan and cook the onion and crushed garlic cloves until soft.

2 Add the pork cubes to the pan and fry until browned. Stir in the caraway seeds, if using, and fresh dill and pour in the stock. Cook for 1 hour over a gentle heat.

3 Stir the drained sauerkraut into the pork with the paprika. Leave to simmer gently for 45 minutes. Add salt, to taste.

4 Garnish the stew with a little more dill and serve with soured cream sprinkled with paprika, with pickled chillies, if liked.

Pork and Garlic Sausage Casserole

This hearty and filling casserole contains a variety of pork cuts. The light ale helps tenderize and flavour the meat.

INGREDIENTS

Serves 6
45ml/3 tbsp sunflower oil
225g/8oz lean, smoked bacon, rinded
   and diced
450g/1lb lean shoulder of pork,
   trimmed and cut into 2.5cm/
   1in cubes
1 large onion, sliced
900g/2lb potatoes, thickly sliced
250ml/8fl oz/1 cup light ale
225g/8oz/2 cups German garlic
   sausage, skinned and sliced
500g/1¼lb/2¼ cups sauerkraut,
   drained
2 red eating apples, cored and sliced
5ml/1 tsp caraway seeds
salt and freshly ground black pepper

1 Preheat the oven to 180°C/350°F/ Gas 4. Heat 30ml/2 tbsp of the oil in a flameproof casserole. Fry the bacon for 2–3 minutes, then lightly brown the cubes of pork. Set aside.

2 Add the remaining oil to the pan and gently cook the onion for 10 minutes, until soft. Return the meat to the pan and add the potatoes.

3 Stir in the ale and bring to the boil. Cover and cook for 45 minutes.

4 Stir in the garlic sausage, drained sauerkraut, sliced apple and caraway seeds. Season with salt and pepper. Return to the oven and cook the casserole for a further 30 minutes, or until the meat is tender.

Veal Roast

Veal is often flattened then layered or rolled around fillings. This mixture of veal, bacon, egg and ham as a filling is delicious.

INGREDIENTS

Serves 4–6

1.5kg/3lb shoulder of veal or lean
   pork, cut into 2cm/³/₄in slices
225g/8oz smoked bacon rashers
175g/6oz sliced ham
4 eggs, beaten
45ml/3 tbsp milk
3 dill pickles, finely diced
115g/4oz/½ cup butter
45ml/3 tbsp plain flour
350ml/12fl oz/1½ cups water or
   chicken stock
salt and freshly ground black pepper
baby carrots, runner beans and dill
   pickle slices, to serve

1 Preheat the oven to 180°C/350°F/ Gas 4. Place the veal or pork between 2 pieces of clear film and pound or flatten into a regular shape using a meat mallet or rolling pin.

2 Top each slice of veal or pork with a layer of bacon and ham. Beat the eggs in a small pan with the milk and stir until the mixture is softly scrambled. Leave to cool a little.

3 Place a layer of the scrambled egg on top of each slice and spread with a knife, then sprinkle on the finely diced dill pickle.

4 Carefully roll up each slice like a Swiss roll. Tie the rolls securely at regular intervals with string.

5 Heat the butter in a large flameproof casserole. Add the meat rolls and brown on all sides. Remove the pan from the heat. Remove the rolls and set aside. Sprinkle the flour into the pan and stir well.

6 Return the pan to the heat and cook the flour mixture until pale brown then slowly add half of the water. Return the meat rolls to the pan and bring to the boil, then put the casserole in the oven for 1³/₄–2 hours to roast slowly, adding the remaining water during cooking if necessary to prevent the veal from drying out.

7 When cooked, leave the rolls to stand for 10 minutes, before serving in slices with the gravy and baby carrots, runner beans and dill pickle.

Hungarian Goulash

Paprika is a distinctive feature of Hungarian cookery. It is a spicy seasoning ground from a variety of sweet red pepper, which has been grown in this area since the end of the 16th century. Shepherds added the spice to their *gulyás*, and fishermen used it in their stews.

INGREDIENTS

Serves 4–6
30ml/2 tbsp vegetable oil or melted lard
2 onions, chopped
900g/2lb braising or stewing steak, trimmed and cubed
1 garlic clove, crushed
generous pinch of caraway seeds
30ml/2 tbsp paprika
1 firm ripe tomato, chopped
2.4 litres/4 pints/10 cups beef stock
2 green peppers, seeded and sliced
450g/1lb potatoes, diced
salt

For the dumplings
2 eggs, beaten
90ml/6 tbsp plain flour, sifted

1 Heat the oil or lard in a large heavy-based pan. Add the onion and cook until soft.

2 Add the beef cubes to the pan and cook for 10 minutes browning gently, stirring frequently to prevent the meat from sticking.

3 Add the garlic, caraway seeds and a little salt to the pan. Remove from the heat and stir in the paprika and tomato. Pour in the beef stock and cook, covered, over a gentle heat for 1–1½ hours, or until tender.

4 Add the peppers and potatoes to the pan and cook for a further 20–25 minutes stirring occasionally.

5 Meanwhile, make the dumplings by mixing the beaten eggs together with the flour and a little salt. With lightly floured hands roll out the dumplings and drop them into the simmering stew for about 2–3 minutes, or until they rise to the surface of the stew. Adjust the seasoning and serve the goulash in warm dishes.

Roast Beef Marinated in Vegetables

This classic Czech dish uses only the best ingredients, including fillet of beef. You could use a sirloin instead, but you should allow a little extra cooking time.

INGREDIENTS

Serves 6

900g/2lb fillet or sirloin
2 rindless bacon rashers,
   finely shredded
2 onions, finely chopped
2 carrots, finely chopped
2 parsnips, finely chopped
225g/8oz/1 cup celeriac or 4 celery
   sticks, finely diced
2 bay leaves
2.5ml/½ tsp allspice
5ml/1 tsp dried thyme
30ml/2 tbsp chopped fresh flat
   leaf parsley
250ml/8 fl oz/1 cup red wine vinegar
60ml/4 tbsp olive oil
50g/2oz/4 tbsp butter
2.5ml/½ tsp sugar
salt and freshly ground black pepper
120ml/4fl oz/½ cup soured cream
flat leaf parsley, to garnish

For the dumplings

6 large potatoes, peeled and quartered
115g/4oz/1 cup plain flour
2 eggs, beaten

1 The day before, lard the beef with strips of bacon and season well.

2 Place the beef in a non-metallic bowl and sprinkle around the vegetables and bay leaves.

3 In another bowl mix together the allspice, thyme, parsley, vinegar and half of the olive oil. Pour this over the beef. Cover with clear film and place in the refrigerator. Leave for 2–3 hours, or longer if possible. Baste the beef occasionally with the marinade.

4 Preheat the oven to 180°C/350°F/ Gas 4. Heat the remaining olive oil in a pan, add the beef and brown all over. Transfer the joint to a large roasting tin. Pour a little water into the pan to de-glaze, stir well, then pour over the meat.

5 Spoon the vegetable marinade around the joint in the roasting tin and dot the top of the meat with the butter. Sprinkle on the sugar. Roast for 1¼–1½ hours, basting occasionally.

--- COOK'S TIP ---

Larding means to insert thins strips of pork or bacon, called lardons, into a cut of meat. This is done to ensure that the cooked meat is moist and tender. Insert the strips with a larding needle or use your fingers.

6 Meanwhile, make the dumplings. Cook the potatoes for 15–20 minutes, drain then mash well. Sprinkle the flour over the potatoes with half the egg and stir well. When all the flour is incorporated add the remaining egg.

7 Turn the potato mixture on to a lightly floured surface and shape into 2 evenly sized oblongs. Bring a pan of salted water to the boil and cook for about 20 minutes. Leave to cool a little before slicing into portions.

8 While the dumplings are cooking remove the joint from the roasting tin and leave to stand before carving. Remove a spoonful of the cooked vegetables and reserve for garnishing. Carefully purée the remaining vegetables and meat juices in a food processor or blender.

9 Reheat the vegetable purée in a pan and season to taste. Add a little extra water if the sauce is too thick. Stir in the soured cream. Serve the beef in slices with the sauce and dumplings and garnish with reserved vegetables and parsley sprigs.

Sauerbraten

The classic sweet-sour marinade gives this dish its name.

INGREDIENTS

Serves 6
1kg/2¼lb silverside of beef
30ml/2 tbsp sunflower oil
1 onion, sliced
115g/4oz smoked streaky bacon, diced
15ml/1 tbsp cornflour
50g/2oz/1 cup crushed ginger biscuits
flat leaf parsley, to garnish
buttered noodles, to serve

For the marinade
2 onions, sliced
1 carrot, sliced
2 celery sticks, sliced
600ml/1 pint/2½ cups water
150ml/¼ pint/⅔ cup red vinegar
1 bay leaf
6 cloves
6 whole black peppercorns
15ml/1 tbsp soft dark brown sugar
10ml/2 tsp salt

1 To make the marinade, put the onions, carrot and celery into a pan with the water. Bring to the boil and simmer for 5 minutes. Add the remaining marinade ingredients and simmer for a further 5 minutes. Cover and leave to cool.

2 Put the joint in a casserole into which it just fits. Pour over the marinade, cover and leave to marinate in the refrigerator for 3 days if possible, turning the joint daily.

3 Remove the joint from the marinade and dry thoroughly using kitchen paper. Heat the oil in a large frying pan and brown the beef over a high heat. Remove the joint and set aside. Add the sliced onion to the pan and fry for 5 minutes. Add the bacon and cook for a further 5 minutes, or until lightly browned.

4 Strain the marinade, reserving the liquid. Put the onion and bacon in a large flameproof casserole or pan, then put the beef on top. Pour over the marinade liquid. Slowly bring to the boil, cover, then simmer over a low heat for 1½–2 hours, or until the beef is very tender.

5 Remove the beef and keep warm. Blend the cornflour in a cup with a little cold water. Add to the cooking liquid with the ginger biscuit crumbs and bring to the boil, stirring. Thickly slice the beef and serve on a bed of hot buttered noodles. Garnish with sprigs of fresh flat leaf parsley and serve the gravy separately.

Chicken with Wild Mushrooms and Garlic

This roasted chicken dish has a hint of fresh herbs.

INGREDIENTS

Serves 4
45ml/3 tbsp olive or vegetable oil
1.5kg/3lb chicken
1 large onion, finely chopped
3 celery sticks, chopped
2 garlic cloves, crushed
275g/10oz/4 cups fresh wild
    mushrooms, sliced if large
5ml/1 tsp chopped fresh thyme
250ml/8fl oz/1 cup chicken stock
250ml/8fl oz/1 cup dry white wine
juice of 1 lemon
30ml/2 tbsp chopped fresh parsley
120ml/4fl oz/¹/₂ cup soured cream
salt and freshly ground black pepper
flat leaf parsley, to garnish
fresh green beans, to serve

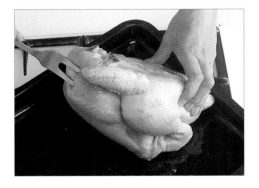

1 Preheat the oven to 190°C/375°F/ Gas 5. Heat the oil in a roasting tin and brown the chicken all over.

2 Add the onion and fry for about 2 minutes. Add the next 4 ingredients and cook for 3 minutes.

3 Pour the chicken stock, wine and lemon juice into the roasting tin. Sprinkle over half of the parsley and season well. Place the chicken in the oven and cook for 1¹/₂–1³/₄ hours, or until tender, basting occasionally to prevent drying out.

— COOK'S TIP —

Clean wild mushrooms well to remove any grit, or use cultured mushrooms instead.

4 Remove the chicken from the roasting tin and keep warm. Put the roasting tin on the hob and stir in the soured cream over a gentle heat, adding a little extra stock or water if necessary to make the juices into a thick pouring sauce.

5 Arrange the chicken on a plate, surrounded by the creamy mushrooms. Garnish with the parsley sprigs and serve the chicken with the sauce and fresh green beans.

Chicken in Badacsonyi Wine

In Hungary, this recipe is made with a Balatan wine called *Badacsonyi Këkryalii* ("Blue Handled"), which has a full body and distinctive bouquet.

INGREDIENTS

Serves 4
50g/2oz/4 tbsp butter
4 spring onions, chopped
115g/4oz rindless smoked
  bacon, diced
2 bay leaves
1 tarragon sprig
1.5kg/3lb cornfed chicken
60ml/4 tbsp sweet sherry or mead
115g/4oz/scant 2 cups button
  mushrooms, sliced
300ml/½ pint/1¼ cups *Badacsonyi*
  or dry white wine
salt
tarragon and bay leaves,
  to garnish
fresh steamed rice, to serve

1 Heat the butter in a large heavy-based pan or flameproof casserole and sweat the spring onions for 1–1½ minutes. Add the bacon, bay leaves and the tarragon, stripping the leaves from the stem. Cook for a further 1 minute.

--- COOK'S TIP ---

Traditionally, this recipe also used a sweet drink with a honeyed caramel flavour called márc. If this is not available, replace it with sweet sherry or mead.

2 Add the whole chicken to the pan and pour in the sweet sherry or mead. Cook, covered, over a very low heat for 15 minutes.

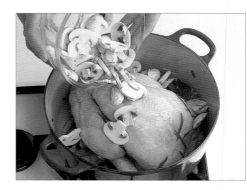

3 Sprinkle the mushrooms into the pan and pour in the wine. Cook, covered, for a further 1 hour. Remove the lid, baste the chicken with the wine mixture and cook, uncovered, for a further 30 minutes, until almost all the liquid has evaporated.

4 Skim the cooking liquid remaining in the pan. Season to taste and remove the chicken, vegetables and bacon to a serving dish. Garnish with tarragon and bay leaves and serve with freshly cooked rice.

Roast Goose with Apples

Ganzebraten mit Apfeln symbolizes Christmas dinner in Germany. Here it is served with hazelnut- and honey-stuffed apples.

INGREDIENTS

Serves 6

115g/4oz/scant 1 cup raisins
finely grated rind and juice of 1 orange
25g/1oz/2 tbsp butter
1 onion, finely chopped
75g/3oz/³/₄ cup hazelnuts, chopped
175g/6oz/3 cups fresh white
　breadcrumbs
15ml/1 tbsp clear honey
15ml/1 tbsp chopped fresh marjoram
30ml/2 tbsp chopped fresh parsley
6 red eating apples
15ml/1 tbsp lemon juice
4.5–5kg/10–11lb oven-ready
　young goose
salt and freshly ground black pepper
fresh herbs, to garnish
orange wedges, red cabbage and green
　beans, to serve

1 Preheat the oven to 220°C/425°F/ Gas 7. Put the raisins in a bowl and pour over the orange juice. Melt the butter in a frying pan and then gently cook the onion for 5 minutes.

2 Add the chopped nuts to the pan and cook for a further 4–5 minutes, or until beginning to brown.

3 Add the cooked onion and nuts to the raisins with 50g/2oz/1 cup of the breadcrumbs, the orange rind, honey, herbs and seasoning. Mix well.

4 Wash the apples and remove the cores to leave a 2cm/³/₄in hole. Using a sharp knife, make a shallow cut around the middle of each apple. Brush the cut and the cavity with the lemon juice to prevent it from browning.

5 Pack the centre of each apple with the nut and raisin stuffing.

6 Mix the remaining breadcrumbs into the stuffing and stuff the bird's tail end. Close with a small skewer.

7 Place the goose in a roasting tin, then prick the skin all over with a skewer. Roast for 30 minutes, then reduce the oven temperature to 180°C/350°F/Gas 4 and cook for a further 3 hours, pouring the excess fat out of the tin several times.

8 Arrange the apples around the goose and bake for 30–40 minutes, or until tender. Rest the goose in a warm place for 15 minutes, before carving. Garnish with fresh herbs, stuffed apples and orange wedges, with red cabbage and green beans.

> COOK'S TIP
>
> To test whether the goose is cooked, pierce the thigh with a thin skewer. The juice that runs out should be pale yellow. If it is tinged with pink, roast the goose for a further 10 minutes and test again.

Fish

Indigenous central European freshwater fish include carp, pike, trout, bream and wels, a type of catfish. A popular saltwater fish is cod. Fresh fish is often baked or poached and served with sauces, such as the German recipe for Cod in Mustard Sauce or the Czech recipe for Carp in Black Sauce. Many of these recipes have remained unchanged for generations – such as Hungarian Fish Sausages dating from the 17th century and German Blue Trout – and are still the best way to appreciate the distinctive flavours of these fish.

Baked Pike with Wild Mushrooms

Pike is a large family of fish found in the rivers of Europe. It has a good, fresh flavour and firm white flesh, making it perfect for baking in a creamy-paprika sauce with wild mushrooms and peppers.

INGREDIENTS

Serves 4–6

about 1.5kg/3lb whole pike
  or perch
115g/4oz/½ cup butter
115g/4oz/½ cup finely sliced onion
225g/8oz/3 cups wild mushrooms,
  roughly sliced
15ml/1 tbsp paprika
25ml/1½ tbsp flour
250ml/8fl oz/1 cup soured cream
15ml/1 tbsp finely chopped
  green pepper
salt and freshly ground black pepper

1 Preheat the oven to 190°C/375°F/ Gas 5. Clean, skin and fillet the fish and put the bones and skin in a large pan. Cover with cold water and bring to the boil. Reduce the heat, season and simmer for 30 minutes.

--- COOK'S TIP ---

Perch or any firm-fleshed white fish can be used instead of pike.

2 Meanwhile, butter a roasting tin, add the fillets and lightly season.

3 Melt the remaining butter in a pan and add the onion. Cook gently for 3–4 minutes, before adding the mushrooms. Cook for a further 2–3 minutes then sprinkle in the paprika.

4 Strain the fish stock, ladle out 250ml/8fl oz/1 cup and pour into the onion and mushrooms.

5 Blend the flour with the soured cream, stir into the pan, then pour over the fish. Bake for 30 minutes or until just tender. Sprinkle the green pepper over the top of the onion and mushroom mixture just before serving.

Carp in Black Sauce

This Czech dish is usually served on Christmas Eve. The carp is generally sold alive and then kept in fresh clean water – often in the bath – until required.

INGREDIENTS

Serves 4
50g/2oz/4 tbsp butter
1 onion, sliced
2 carrots, diced
2 small parsnips, diced
¼ small celeriac, diced
juice of 1 lemon
50ml/2fl oz/¼ cup red wine vinegar
175ml/6fl oz/¾ cup dark ale
8 whole black peppercorns
2.5ml/½ tsp allspice
1 bay leaf
5ml/1 tsp chopped fresh thyme
2cm/¾in piece of root ginger, peeled and grated
1 strip of lemon peel
3 slices of dark pumpernickel bread, processed into crumbs
30ml/2 tbsp flour
15ml/1 tbsp sugar
40g/1½oz/⅓ cup raisins
6 ready-to-eat prunes
30ml/2 tbsp hazelnuts and almonds, roughly chopped
4 thick carp or sea bream steaks
salt and freshly ground black pepper
fresh snipped chives, to garnish
dumplings and fresh bread, to serve

1 Melt half of the butter in a flame-proof casserole. Add the onion and cook for 2–3 minutes, then stir in the carrots, parsnips and celeriac. Cook for a further 5 minutes.

2 Stir in the lemon juice, red wine vinegar and dark ale. Pour in just enough water to cover.

3 Place the peppercorns, allspice, bay leaf, thyme, ginger, lemon peel and a little seasoning, in a bowl. Stir in the breadcrumbs, mix well and add to the vegetables. Simmer for 15 minutes.

4 Meanwhile, melt the remaining butter in a small pan and sprinkle in the flour. Cook gently for 1–2 minutes before adding the sugar. Cook for a further 2–3 minutes or until the sugar caramelizes.

5 Gradually ladle all of the stock from the casserole into the flour mixture; stir well then pour this back into the vegetable mixture. Add the raisins, prunes and nuts, and seasoning.

6 Place the fish steaks on top of the vegetables and cook for 12–15 minutes. To serve, arrange the fish on dishes, strain the vegetables, nuts and fruit and place them around the fish. Reduce the sauce by boiling quickly. Garnish with snipped chives and serve with dumplings and fresh bread.

Fish Goulash

This wholesome meal is a cross between a stew and a soup. It is traditionally served with a hot cherry pepper in the centre of the serving plate and the goulash ladled over it.

INGREDIENTS

Serves 6
2kg/4¹/₂lb mixed fish
4 large onions, sliced
2 garlic cloves, crushed
¹/₂ small celeriac, diced
handful of parsley stalks or
   cleaned roots
30ml/2 tbsp paprika
1 green pepper, seeded and sliced
5–10ml/1–2 tsp tomato purée
salt
90ml/6 tbsp soured cream and
   3 cherry peppers (optional),
   to serve

1 Skin and fillet the fish and cut the flesh into chunks. Put all the fish heads, skin and bones into a large pan, together with the onions, garlic, celeriac, parsley stalks, paprika and salt. Cover with water and bring to the boil. Reduce the heat and simmer for 1¹/₄ –1¹/₂ hours. Strain the stock.

2 Place the fish and green pepper in a large frying pan and pour over the stock. Blend the tomato purée with a little stock and pour it into the pan.

3 Heat gently but do not stir, or the fish will break up. Cook for just 10–12 minutes but do not boil. Season to taste. Ladle into warmed deep plates or bowls and top with a generous spoonful of soured cream and a halved cherry pepper, if liked.

Fish Sausages

This recipe has featured in many Hungarian cookbooks since the 17th century.

INGREDIENTS

Serves 3–4
375g/13oz fish fillets, such as perch,
   pike, carp, cod, skinned
1 white bread roll
75ml/5 tbsp milk
25ml/1¹/₂ tbsp chopped fresh flat
   leaf parsley
2 eggs, well beaten
50g/2oz/¹/₂ cup plain flour
50g/2oz/1 cup fine fresh
   white breadcrumbs
oil, for shallow frying
salt and freshly ground black pepper
deep fried sprigs of parsley and lemon
   wedges, sprinkled with paprika,
   to serve

1 Mince or process the fish coarsely in a food processor or blender. Soak the roll in the milk for about 10 minutes, then squeeze it out. Mix the fish and bread together before adding the chopped parsley, one of the eggs and seasoning.

2 Using your fingers, shape the mixture into 10cm/4in long sausages, about 2.5cm/1in thick.

3 Carefully roll the fish "sausages" into the flour, then in the remaining egg and then lastly in the breadcrumbs.

4 Heat the oil in a pan then slowly cook the "sausages" until golden brown all over. Drain well on crumpled kitchen paper. Garnish with deep fried parsley sprigs and lemon wedges sprinkled with paprika.

Halibut Cooked Under a Mountain of Cream

Halibut steaks are lightly cooked with bacon and wine, smothered in cream sauce and flash-grilled.

INGREDIENTS

Serves 4
1 small onion, chopped
4 parsley sprigs
1 bay leaf
6 whole black peppercorns
150ml/¼ pint/⅔ cup white wine
8 lean streaky bacon rashers, rinded
4 halibut steaks, about 900g/2lb
 in total
10ml/2 tsp plain flour
15g/½ oz/1 tbsp butter, softened
1.5ml/¼ tsp salt
pinch of paprika
120ml/4fl oz/½ cup double cream,
 lightly whipped
25g/1oz/⅓ cup grated Parmesan
sage leaves, to garnish
Parmesan, paprika and lemon, to serve

1 Preheat the oven to 180°C/350°F/ Gas 4. Put the onion, parsley, bay leaf, whole black peppercorns and wine in a small pan. Bring to the boil, then cover and simmer for 15 minutes. Leave to cool.

2 Cook the bacon rashers in a non-stick frying pan until lightly browned. Arrange the fish steaks in a greased shallow ovenproof dish. Place the bacon on top.

3 Strain the infused wine into the dish through a sieve, discarding the cooked onion and herbs. Bake in the oven for 12–15 minutes, or until the fish is just cooked.

4 Remove and reserve the bacon rashers. Strain the fish cooking liquid into a pan, again through a sieve, and bring to the boil.

5 Blend the flour and the butter to a paste in a small bowl. Whisk into the pan of stock and simmer for 3–4 minutes. Season with salt and paprika. Fold the cream into the sauce.

6 Transfer the fish to serving plates. Pour the sauce over the fish and sprinkle with the grated Parmesan. Place under a preheated medium grill for 3–4 minutes, or until lightly browned. Serve straight away, sprinkled with the reserved bacon cut into strips and garnished with sage leaves. Serve with extra Parmesan, paprika and lemon slices.

Baked Carp

Indigenous to the area, carp is a major ingredient in Hungarian cooking. It has a sweet, firm flesh that tastes wonderful when baked with bacon and bay leaves.

INGREDIENTS

Serves 4–6
450g/1lb old potatoes, scrubbed
115g/4oz rindless smoked bacon
about 900g/2lb whole carp, skinned,
    filleted and cut into 7.5cm/3in pieces
8–12 bay leaves
15ml/1 tbsp lard
1 onion, thinly sliced
15ml/1 tbsp paprika
1 large tomato, sliced
2 green peppers, seeded and sliced
40g/1½oz/3 tbsp butter, melted
150ml/¼ pint/⅔ cup soured cream
salt
bay leaves, to garnish

1 Preheat the oven to 190°C/375°F/ Gas 5. Boil the potatoes in their skins in a pan of boiling salted water for 15–20 minutes. Drain the potatoes and slice them.

2 Meanwhile, cut the bacon into strips. Make incisions in the fillets and push in the bacon and bay leaves.

COOK'S TIP

Pungent, salty bacon is a great partner for white fish: this is a combination found in many European cuisines.

3 Put the potatoes in a large well- buttered casserole. Add salt.

4 Melt the lard and fry the onion slices for 1–2 minutes. Stir in the paprika. Arrange the onion on the potato slices.

5 Place a layer of tomato and peppers on top of the onion then add the fish and a little salt.

6 Pour the melted butter over the fish. Bake in the oven for 30 minutes. Pour over the soured cream and cook for a further 15 minutes. Serve garnished with bay leaves.

Blue Trout

The blue sheen of *Blaue Forelle* is a German speciality and is easily achieved by first scalding the fish and then fanning to cool it. Traditionally the fish was left to cool in a breeze or draught.

INGREDIENTS

Serves 4

4 trout, about 175g/6oz each
5ml/1 tsp salt
600ml/1 pint/2½ cups white
    wine vinegar
1 onion, sliced
2 bay leaves
6 whole black peppercorns
bay leaves and lemon slices, to garnish
115g/4oz/½ cup melted butter,
    creamed horseradish sauce and green
    beans, to serve

1 Preheat the oven to 180°C/350°F/ Gas 4. Rub both sides of the trout with salt and place in a non–aluminium roasting tin or fish kettle.

2 Bring the vinegar to the boil and slowly pour over the trout. Fan the fish as it cools or leave to stand in a draught for 5 minutes.

3 Bring the vinegar back to the boil, then add the sliced onion, bay leaves and peppercorns.

4 Cover the tin with foil and cook in the oven for 30 minutes, or until the fish is cooked. Transfer the fish to warmed serving dishes, garnish with bay leaves and lemon slices, and serve with melted butter, creamed horseradish sauce and green beans.

Baked Salmon

This Czech recipe uses freshwater fish such as salmon or trout but saltwater fish such as mackerel can also be used. It is a very simple but tasty meal as the fish cooks in its own juices.

INGREDIENTS

Serves 6

1.75kg/4lb whole salmon
115g/4oz/½ cup butter, melted
2.5–5ml/½–1 tsp caraway seeds
45ml/3 tbsp lemon juice
salt and freshly ground pepper
sprigs of flat leaf parsley and lemon
    wedges, to garnish

COOK'S TIP

Take care when cutting the fish: dip your fingers into a little salt to help you to grip the fish better.

1 Preheat the oven to 180°C/350°F/ Gas 4. Using a sharp knife, cut the fish in half lengthways.

2 Place the salmon, skin side down, in a lightly greased roasting tin and brush with the melted butter. Season, sprinkle over the caraway seeds and then the lemon juice.

3 Bake the salmon in the oven, loosely covered with foil, for 25 minutes or until the flesh flakes easily.

4 Transfer the fish to a serving plate. Garnish with flat leaf parsley and lemon wedges. Serve hot or cold.

Marinated Fish

With a number of tart flavours, this is a strong, zesty marinade.

INGREDIENTS

Serves 6–8

1.75kg/4lb tuna, carp or pike steaks
75g/3oz/6 tbsp butter, melted
50ml/2fl oz/¼ cup dry sherry
salt and freshly ground black pepper

For the marinade

400ml/14fl oz/1⅔ cups water
150ml/¼ pint/⅔ cup wine vinegar
150ml/¼ pint/⅔ cup good fish stock
1 onion, thinly sliced
6 white peppercorns
2.5ml/½ tsp allspice
2 cloves
1 bay leaf
25ml/1½ tbsp bottled capers, drained and chopped
2 dill pickles, diced
120ml/4fl oz/½ cup olive oil
salad, dill pickles and bread, to serve

1 Preheat the oven to 180°C/350°F/ Gas 4. Put the fish steaks into an ovenproof dish and brush with the butter. Sprinkle over the sherry. Season well and bake for 20–25 minutes, or until just tender. Leave to cool.

2 Meanwhile, boil the water, vinegar, fish stock, onion, spices and bay leaf together in a pan for 20 minutes. Leave to cool before adding the capers, dill pickle and olive oil.

COOK'S TIP

Use plump fillets of fish if tuna steaks are not available.

3 Once the fish steaks have cooled pour over the marinade.

4 Cover the dish with clear film and leave to marinate the fish for 24 hours in the refrigerator, basting occasionally. Serve with a green salad, dill pickles and slices of pumpernickel or rye bread.

Cod in Mustard Sauce

A firm, white-fleshed fish, cod is abundant in the North Sea and features in many German recipes. Reduced stock sauces, as in this dish, are tending to replace the heavier flour-based versions of former times.

INGREDIENTS

Serves 4

900g/2lb cod fillets
1 lemon
1 small onion, sliced
15g/½oz/¼ cup chopped fresh flat
  leaf parsley, whole stalks reserved
6 allspice berries
6 whole black peppercorns
1 clove
1 bay leaf
1.2 litres/2 pints/5 cups water
30ml/2 tbsp wholegrain mustard
75g/3oz/6 tbsp butter
salt and freshly ground black pepper
bay leaves, to garnish
boiled potatoes and carrots,
  to serve

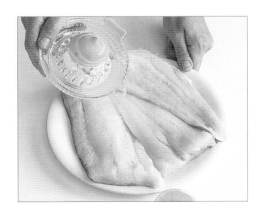

1 Place the fish on a plate. Pare two thin strips of rind from the lemon, then squeeze the lemon for its juice. Sprinkle the juice over the fish.

2 Put the lemon rind in a large frying pan with the onion, the stalks from the parsley, the allspice, peppercorns, clove and bay leaf.

3 Pour in the water. Slowly bring to the boil, cover and simmer for 20 minutes. Add the fish, cover and cook *very* gently for 10 minutes.

4 Ladle 250ml/8fl oz/1 cup of the cooking liquid into a pan and simmer until reduced by half. Stir in the mustard.

5 Whisk the butter, a little at a time, into the reduced stock. Taste and season with salt and pepper, if needed.

6 Remove the fish from the stock and place on warmed serving dishes. Pour over a little sauce and serve the rest separately in a jug. Garnish with chopped parsley and bay leaves and serve with boiled potatoes and carrots.

VEGETABLES, GRAINS AND PASTA

Home-grown vegetables form part of the local economy in much of rural central Europe. Vegetables may be pickled to preserve them throughout the year or used fresh in many interesting ways. Potatoes form an important part of the diet – served hot, made into potato cakes or eaten cold in salads. More popular in southern Germany is a pasta dish called Spätzle. Dried beans and pulses can be served on their own or as part of a main meal to extend the protein in dishes, particularly in Czech and Hungarian cooking.

Potato Salad

Use either new or waxy potatoes for this classic East European salad, since they will hold their shape when cooked.

INGREDIENTS

Serves 6
750g/1½ lb potatoes, scrubbed
45ml/3 tbsp olive oil
4 smoked streaky bacon rashers, rinded
  and chopped
10ml/2 tsp lemon juice
2 celery sticks, chopped
2 pickled sour cucumbers, diced
5ml/1 tsp Dusseldorf or German
  mustard
45ml/3 tbsp mayonnaise
30ml/2 tbsp snipped fresh chives
15ml/1 tbsp chopped fresh dill
salt and freshly ground pepper
fresh chives and dill,
  to garnish

1 Cook the potatoes in a pan of boiling salted water for 15 minutes, until just tender. Drain, allow to cool for 5 minutes, then slice thickly and set aside in a bowl.

--- COOK'S TIP ---

German mustard is typically dark with a medium heat and a slightly sweet flavour; it is an ideal accompaniment for sausages, ham and bacon.

2 Meanwhile, heat 15ml/1 tbsp of the oil in a frying pan and fry the bacon for 5 minutes, until crispy. Remove the bacon and set aside.

3 Stir the remaining oil and lemon juice into the pan then pour over the sliced warm potatoes. Add the celery, cucumber and half the bacon and mix well. Leave to cool.

4 Blend the mustard in a small bowl with the mayonnaise, herbs and a little seasoning. Add to the potatoes and toss well to coat. Spoon the potatoes into a serving dish and sprinkle with the remaining bacon. Garnish with the fresh herbs and serve with lettuce leaves.

Himmel und Erde

This dish from the Rhineland, whose name translates as "heaven and earth", combines apples "from heaven" and potatoes "from the earth", and is served with slices of black pudding and crisp onion rings.

INGREDIENTS

Serves 4

450g/1lb floury potatoes, peeled and quartered
350g/12oz cooking apples, cored, peeled and chopped
50g/2oz/4 tbsp butter
2 cloves
pinch of nutmeg
30ml/2 tbsp sunflower oil
350g/12oz *blutwurst* (black pudding), cut into 1cm/½in slices
1 onion, sliced into rings
salt and freshly ground black pepper

1 Cook the potatoes in a pan of boiling salted water for 20 minutes, or until tender. Drain well.

2 Meanwhile, put the chopped apples and 15g/½oz/1 tbsp of the butter in a small pan with the cloves. Cook gently for 10 minutes, until soft.

3 Discard the cloves then add the cooked apple to the potato with the remaining butter, nutmeg and a little salt and pepper.

4 Mash the mixture until smooth and creamy. Pile on to a serving plate and keep warm.

5 Meanwhile heat the oil in a frying pan and cook the black pudding for 5 minutes, or until crisp. Remove from the pan with a slotted spoon and arrange to one side of the purée.

6 Add the onion rings to the pan and fry for 12–15 minutes, until lightly browned and crispy. Pile on top of the purée and serve hot.

Kohlrabi Baked with Ham

Kohlrabi, which is German for "cabbage-turnip", is a member of the cabbage family with a delicate turnip-like taste. Kohlrabi may be purple or greenish-white and is delicious either raw, grated and sprinkled with salt, or cooked. The leaves can also be eaten – treat in the same way as spinach.

INGREDIENTS

Serves 4
50g/2oz/4 tbsp butter
4 kohlrabi, peeled and diced
225g/8oz thick ham, diced
30ml/2 tbsp chopped fresh parsley

For the sauce
3 egg yolks
250ml/8fl oz/1 cup double cream
30ml/2 tbsp plain flour
pinch of mace
salt and freshly ground black pepper

1 Preheat the oven to 180°C/350°F/ Gas 4. Melt the butter in a large frying pan and gently cook the kohlrabi for 8–10 minutes.

2 Arrange half of the kohlrabi in the bottom of a greased ovenproof dish. Top with the ham and parsley, and finish with the remaining kohlrabi.

---- COOK'S TIP ----

Choose the smallest kohlrabi you can find, as these will have the freshest flavour.

3 Beat the sauce ingredients together and pour over the kohlrabi and ham. Bake for 30–35 minutes or until golden brown, and serve hot.

Poached Celery

This simple but tasty way of presenting celery is one that can also be used for kohlrabi, cauliflower or leeks. Select a hard cheese with a medium to vintage flavour.

INGREDIENTS

Serves 4
4 celery hearts
25g/1oz/2 tbsp butter
250ml/8fl oz/1 cup dry white wine
salt and freshly ground black pepper
15ml/1 tbsp chopped fresh parsley, to garnish
grated cheese, to serve

1 Scrub the celery well and trim the ends. Cut the celery hearts in half lengthways.

2 Parboil or blanch the celery in a pan of boiling salted water for 5 minutes. Drain and rinse quickly under cold water. Gently pat dry with kitchen paper.

3 Melt the butter in a frying pan and gently cook the celery for 1–2 minutes. Pour in the wine and bring to the boil. Reduce the heat to a simmer.

4 Cook uncovered for 5 minutes or until just tender. Drain well. Sprinkle with parsley and black pepper and serve with grated cheese on top.

Somogy Beans

This recipe comes from Somogy in Hungary, but every region has its own speciality. Serve with roast chicken, if liked.

Ingredients

Serves 6–8

450g/1lb/2½ cups dried white beans, such as haricots or white kidney beans, soaked overnight
1 bay leaf
225g/8oz piece of lean smoked rindless bacon
15g/½oz/1 tbsp lard
1 onion, very finely chopped
2 garlic cloves, crushed
15ml/1 tbsp plain flour
15–30ml/1–2 tbsp vinegar
generous pinch of sugar
120ml/4fl oz/½ cup soured cream
salt
sage leaves and paprika, to garnish

1 Drain the white beans already soaked overnight and rinse well.

2 Put the beans in a large pan with the bay leaf, bacon and water to cover. Cook for about 1¼–1½ hours, or until the beans are tender. Carefully remove the bacon and dice when cool. Drain the beans, reserving 120ml/4fl oz/½ cup of the cooking liquid. (It may be useful to reserve a little more than this, in case it is needed in Step 5.)

3 Melt the lard in a frying pan and stir in the onion, garlic and flour. Cook for 2–3 minutes, then slowly stir in the reserved cooking liquid. Stir well.

4 Return the beans to a pan. Add the bacon and onion and stir well.

5 Add the vinegar, sugar and soured cream to the pan. Season to taste. If required, add a little more cooking liquid if the bean mixture is too stiff. Garnish with sage leaves and paprika.

COOK'S TIP

Salt is added only at the end of this recipe, otherwise the beans become tough.

Lecsó

Like much of Eastern Europe, Hungary makes good use of its fresh produce. Many of its vegetable recipes are substantial, flavoursome dishes, intended to be eaten by themselves, as with this recipe, and not just as an accompaniment to meat, poultry or fish dishes.

Lecsó, in its most basic form of a thick tomato and onion purée, is also used as the basis for stews and other dishes.

INGREDIENTS

Serves 6–8
5 green peppers
30ml/2 tbsp vegetable oil or
   melted lard
1 onion, sliced
450g/1lb plum tomatoes, peeled
   and chopped
15ml/1 tbsp paprika
sugar and salt, to taste
grilled bacon strips, to garnish
crusty bread, to serve

3 Add the strips of pepper and cook gently for 10 minutes.

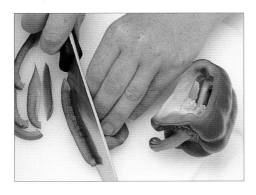

1 Wipe the green peppers, remove the cores and seeds and slice the flesh into strips.

2 Heat the oil or lard. Add the onion and cook over a low heat for 5 minutes until just softened.

4 Add the chopped tomatoes and paprika and season to taste with a little sugar and salt.

5 Simmer the ratatouille over a low heat for 20–25 minutes. Serve immediately, topped with the strips of grilled bacon and accompanied by crusty bread.

— VARIATION —

To vary this recipe add 115g/4oz/1 cup sliced salami, or some lightly scrambled eggs to the vegetables.

Hot Cheese Pastries

One of many recipes for cheese pastries, often served to guests with Hungarian wine.

Ingredients

Makes about 30
400g/14oz packet puff pastry, thawed
1 large egg, beaten
115–150g/4–5oz Liptauer cheese (see Cook's Tip), finely crumbled

---
Cook's Tip

Hungarian *liptauer* is a cheese spread made from a white sheep's milk cheese, *liptó*, spiced with paprika, salt and various other ingredients, such as onion, caraway seeds, mustard and capers. *Liptauer* has a heady, spicy flavour. If unavailable, use feta cheese or the Romanian *brinza* instead.

1 Preheat the oven to 200°C/400°F/ Gas 6. Roll out the puff pastry on a lightly floured surface to a 30cm/12in long oblong about 5mm/¼in thick. Cut the pastry in half crossways.

2 Glaze the pastry with the beaten egg, sprinkle over the Liptauer cheese and push it lightly into the pastry. Cut the pastry into 15 × 2.5cm/ 6 × 1in strips.

3 Twist the pastry strips to form long spiral shapes. Place on a non-stick baking sheet and bake for 10–15 minutes, or until golden brown. Cool on a wire rack.

Bavarian Potato Dumplings

The cuisines of Germany and Central Europe are unimaginable without dumplings, consumed in all shapes and sizes. In this version, crunchy croûtons are placed in the centre.

Ingredients

Serves 6
1.5kg/3lb potatoes, peeled
115g/4oz/⅔ cup semolina
115g/4oz/1 cup wholemeal flour
5ml/1 tsp salt
1.5ml/¼ tsp nutmeg
30ml/2 tbsp sunflower oil
2 thin white bread slices, crusts removed, cubed
1.5 litres/2½ pints/6¼ cups beef stock
freshly ground black pepper
chopped fresh flat leaf parsley, crispy bacon and onion slices, to garnish
melted butter, to serve

1 Cook the potatoes in a large pan of boiling salted water for 20 minutes, or until tender. Drain well, then mash and press through a sieve into a bowl. Add the semolina, flour, salt, a little pepper and the nutmeg and mix well.

2 Heat the oil in a frying pan and fry the cubes of bread until light golden brown. Drain the croûtons on kitchen paper.

3 Divide the potato mixture into 24 balls. Press a few of the fried croûtons firmly into each dumpling. Bring the stock to the boil in a large pan, add the dumplings and cook gently for 5 minutes, turning once.

4 Remove the dumplings with a slotted spoon and arrange on a warmed serving dish. Sprinkle with chopped parsley, crispy bacon and fried onion slices and serve with a jug of melted butter.

Spiced Red Cabbage

Cook this a day before serving. It is a perfect accompaniment to roast pork or game.

INGREDIENTS

Serves 6–8

3 thick rindless bacon rashers, diced
1 large onion, chopped
1 large red cabbage,
  evenly shredded
3 garlic cloves, crushed
15–25ml/1–1½ tbsp caraway seeds
120ml/4 fl oz/½ cup water
2 firm, ripe pears, cored and
  evenly chopped
juice of 1 lemon
475ml/16fl oz/2 cups red wine
45ml/3 tbsp red wine vinegar
150g/5oz/scant ¾ cup clear honey
salt and freshly ground black pepper
caraway seeds and snipped fresh chives,
  to garnish

1 Dry fry the diced bacon in a pan over a gentle heat for 5–10 minutes, or until golden brown.

2 Stir in the onion and cook for 5 minutes or until pale golden.

3 Stir the cabbage, garlic, caraway seeds and the water into the pan. Cover and cook for 8–10 minutes.

4 Season well, then add the pears, lemon juice, red wine and vinegar. Cover and cook for 10–15 minutes. Stir in the honey.

5 If there is too much cooking liquid, remove the lid and allow it to reduce. The pears will have broken up in the pot, and the quantity reduced by one-third. Adjust the seasoning to taste and serve sprinkled with caraway seeds and snipped fresh chives.

Spätzle

This simple pasta dish comes from Swabia in south-west Germany, where it is more popular than potatoes and is served with many savoury dishes.

INGREDIENTS

Serves 4

350g/12oz/3 cups plain flour
2.5ml/½ tsp salt
2 eggs, beaten
about 200ml/7fl oz/scant 1 cup milk
   and water combined
15ml/1 tbsp sunflower oil
25g/1oz/2 tbsp butter, melted, plus
   diced bacon, poached celery hearts
   and freshly ground black pepper,
   to serve

1 Sift the flour and salt into a bowl and make a well in the centre. Add the eggs and enough of the milk and water to make a very soft dough.

2 Beat the dough until it develops bubbles, then stir in the oil and beat again. Bring a large pan of salted water to the boil.

3 Dampen a chopping board with water and place the dough on it. Shave off strips of the dough into the water using the broad side of a knife.

COOK'S TIP

Rinse the knife with water occasionally at Step 3, so that the dough does not stick to it. The faster you work at this stage, the lighter the texture of the *spätzle*.

4 Cook for 3 minutes, then remove the pieces with a slotted spoon. Rinse quickly in hot water and put in a warmed serving bowl and cover to keep warm. Repeat until all the dough has been used up.

5 Drizzle the melted butter over the top and serve immediately, topped with diced bacon. Serve with poached celery hearts, and sprinkled with freshly ground black pepper.

DESSERTS AND BAKES

Hungary, Germany and Austria are well known for an impressive range of cakes and desserts, an enviable excellence in the art of pastry-making and an accompanying café culture, which is famous world-wide. It is hard to know which is the greater delight – a slice of rich Black Forest Cherry Cake or melt-in-the-mouth Apple Strudel. Locally grown cherries, plums, apricots and nuts are typical ingredients, while apples appear widely in German desserts and, in particular, baked goods.

Black Forest Cherry Cake

Surprisingly, this famous and much-loved cake is a fairly recent invention. It comes from southern Germany where Kirsch is distilled.

INGREDIENTS

Serves 12
200g/7oz plain chocolate, broken into squares
115g/4oz/½ cup unsalted butter
3 eggs, separated
115g/4oz/½ cup soft dark brown sugar
45ml/3 tbsp Kirsch
75g/3oz/²⁄₃ cup self-raising flour, sifted
50g/2oz/½ cup ground almonds

For the filling and topping
65g/2½ oz plain chocolate
65g/2½ oz plain chocolate-flavoured cake covering
45ml/3 tbsp Kirsch
425g/15oz can stoned black cherries, drained and juice reserved
600ml/1 pint/2½ cups double cream, lightly whipped
12 fresh cherries with stalks

1 Preheat the oven to 180°C/350°F/ Gas 4. Grease and base-line a deep 20cm/8in round cake tin with greased greaseproof paper. Melt the plain chocolate and butter in a heatproof bowl set over a pan of simmering water, stirring to mix. Remove from the heat and leave until barely warm.

2 Whisk the egg yolks and sugar in a bowl until very thick, then fold in the chocolate mixture and the Kirsch. Fold in the flour with the ground almonds. Whisk the egg whites in a grease-free bowl until stiff, then gently fold into the mixture.

3 Pour the mixture into the prepared cake tin and bake in the oven for 40 minutes, or until firm to the touch.

4 Allow the sponge to cool in the tin for 5 minutes, then turn out and cool on a wire rack. Use a long serrated knife to cut the cake horizontally into 3 even layers.

5 Meanwhile, make the chocolate curls. Melt the chocolate and chocolate cake covering in a heatproof bowl set over a pan of simmering water, as before. Cool for 5 minutes, then pour on to a board to set. Use a potato peeler to shave off thin curls.

6 Mix the Kirsch with 90ml/6tbsp of the reserved cherry juice. Place the bottom layer of sponge on a serving plate and sprinkle with 45ml/3 tbsp of the Kirsch syrup.

7 Spread one-third of the whipped cream over the sponge layer and scatter over half the cherries. Place the second layer of sponge on top and repeat with another third of the Kirsch syrup and cream and the remaining cherries. Place the final sponge layer on top and sprinkle the remaining Kirsch syrup over it.

8 Spread the remaining cream over the top of the cake. Sprinkle over the chocolate curls and top with the fresh cherries.

Apple Strudel

This classic recipe is usually made with strudel dough, but filo pastry makes a good shortcut.

INGREDIENTS

Serves 8–10
500g/1¼lb packet large sheets of filo
    pastry, thawed if frozen
115g/4oz/½ cup unsalted butter,
    melted
icing sugar, for dredging
cream, to serve

For the filling

1kg/2¼lb apples, cored, peeled
    and sliced
115g/4oz/2 cups fresh breadcrumbs
50g/2oz/4 tbsp unsalted butter, melted
150g/5oz/¾ cup sugar
5ml/1 tsp cinnamon
75g/3oz/generous ½ cup raisins
finely grated rind of 1 lemon

1 Preheat the oven to 180°C/350°F/ Gas 4. For the filling, place the sliced apples in a bowl. Stir in the breadcrumbs, butter, sugar, cinnamon, raisins and grated lemon rind.

2 Lay 1 or 2 sheets of pastry on a floured surface and brush with melted butter. Place another 1 or 2 sheets on top, and continue until there are 4–5 layers in all.

3 Put the apple on the pastry, with a 2.5cm/1in border all around.

4 Fold in the two shorter sides to enclose the filling, then roll up like a Swiss roll. Place the strudel on a lightly buttered baking sheet.

5 Brush the pastry with the remaining butter. Bake for 30–40 minutes or until golden brown. Leave to cool before dusting with icing sugar. Serve in thick diagonal slices.

Linzertorte

This sweet recipe was named not, as is commonly thought, after the town of Linz, but after Linzer, chef to the Archduke Charles, victor over Napoleon at Aspern in 1809.

INGREDIENTS

Serves 8–10
200g/7oz/scant 1 cup butter
   or margarine
200g/7oz/1 cup caster sugar
3 eggs, beaten
1 egg yolk
2.5ml/½ tsp cinnamon
grated rind of ½ lemon
115g/4oz/2 cups fine sweet
   biscuit crumbs
150g/5oz/1¼ cups ground almonds
225g/8oz/2 cups plain flour, sifted
225g/8oz/¾ cup raspberry jam
1 egg yolk, for glazing
icing sugar, to decorate

1 Preheat the oven to 190°C/375°F/ Gas 5. Cream the butter or margarine and sugar together in a mixing bowl until light and creamy. Add the eggs and egg yolk slowly, beating all the time, before adding the cinnamon and the lemon rind.

2 Stir the biscuit crumbs and ground almonds into the mixture. Mix well together before adding the sifted flour. Knead the pastry mixture lightly, then wrap it in clear film and allow to chill for 30 minutes.

3 Roll out two-thirds of the pastry on a lightly floured surface and use to line a deep 25cm/10in loose-based flan tin. Smooth down the surface.

4 Spread the raspberry jam over the base of the pastry case. Roll out the remaining pastry into a long oblong. Cut this into strips and arrange in a lattice pattern over the jam.

5 Brush the pastry with the beaten egg yolk to glaze. Bake the flan for 35–50 minutes, or until golden brown. Leave to cool in the tin before turning out on to a wire rack. Serve warm or cold with custard and sift over a little icing sugar.

— COOK'S TIP —

Sieve an extra 60ml/4 tbsp warmed raspberry jam and brush over the tart when cold.

Dobos Torta

This well-known cake was first created by a chef called Jozep Dobos in the late 1880s. His famous delicacy was soon exported worldwide in his specially designed packaging. Other cooks failed to replicate this treat, so in 1906 Dobos Makers donated his recipe to the Budapest Pastry and Honey-bread Makers Guild.

INGREDIENTS

Serves 10–12

6 eggs, separated
150g/5oz/1¼ cups icing
   sugar, sifted
5ml/1 tsp vanilla sugar
130g/4½oz/generous 1 cup plain
   flour, sifted

For the filling

75g/3oz plain chocolate, broken
   into pieces
175g/6oz/¾ cup unsalted butter
130g/4½oz/generous 1 cup
   icing sugar
30ml/2 tbsp vanilla sugar
1 egg

For the caramel topping

150g/5oz/¾ cup sugar
30–45ml/2–3 tbsp water
10g/¼oz/½ tbsp butter, melted

1 Preheat the oven to 220°C/425°F/ Gas 7. Whisk the egg yolks and half the icing sugar together in a bowl until pale in colour, thick and creamy.

2 Whisk the egg whites in a grease-free bowl until stiff; whisk in half the remaining icing sugar until glossy, then fold in the vanilla sugar.

3 Fold the egg whites into the egg yolk mixture, alternating carefully with spoonfuls of the flour.

4 Line 4 baking sheets with parchment or greaseproof paper. Draw a 23cm/9in circle on each piece of paper. Lightly grease the paper and dust with flour.

5 Spread the mixture evenly on the paper circles. Bake for 10 minutes, then leave to cool before layering and weighing them down with a board.

6 To make the filling, melt the chocolate in a small heatproof bowl set over a pan of gently simmering water. Stir until smooth.

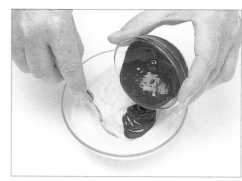

7 Cream the butter and icing sugar together well in a bowl. Beat in the melted chocolate, vanilla sugar and egg.

8 Sandwich the 4 sponge circles together with the chocolate cream filling, then spread the remainder of the cream over the top and around the sides of the cake.

9 To make the caramel topping, put the sugar and water in a heavy-based pan and dissolve slowly over a very gentle heat. Add the butter.

10 When the sugar has dissolved, increase the heat and cook until the mixture turns golden brown. Quickly pour the caramel on to a greased baking sheet. Leave to set and shatter into shards when cold. Place the pieces of caramel on top of the cake, and cut it into slices to serve.

Baked Cheesecake with Kisel

This creamy cheesecake contrasts well with the flavour of fresh or stewed fruit, so why not try it with *kisel*? Originally a German recipe, the red-berry compôte became associated with Russia, where it was introduced by German governesses last century and is still a popular nursery food today.

INGREDIENTS

Serves 8–10
225g/8oz/2 cups plain flour
115g/4oz/½ cup butter
15g/½oz/1 tbsp caster sugar
finely grated rind of ½ lemon
1 egg, beaten
sprigs of mint, to decorate

For the filling
675g/1½lb/3 cups quark
4 eggs, separated
150g/5oz/¾ cup caster sugar
45ml/3 tbsp cornflour
150ml/¼ pint/⅔ cup soured cream
finely grated rind and juice of
  ½ lemon
5ml/1 tsp vanilla essence

For the kisel
450g/1lb/4–4½ cups prepared red
  fruit, such as strawberries,
  raspberries, red currants, cherries
50g/2oz/¼ cup caster sugar
120ml/4fl oz/½ cup water
15ml/1 tbsp arrowroot

1 Begin by making the pastry for the cheesecake. Sift the flour into a bowl. Rub in the butter until the mixture resembles fine breadcrumbs. Stir in the caster sugar and lemon rind, then add the beaten egg and mix to a dough. Wrap in clear film and chill for at least 15 minutes.

2 Roll out the pastry on a lightly floured surface and use to line the base and sides of a 25cm/10in loose-bottomed cake tin. Chill for 1 hour.

3 Put the quark for the filling in a fine sieve set over a bowl and leave to drain for 1 hour.

4 Preheat the oven to 200°C/400°F/Gas 6. Prick the chilled pastry case base with a fork, fill it with crumpled foil and bake for 5 minutes. Remove the foil and bake for a further 5 minutes. Remove the pastry case from the oven and reduce the oven temperature to 180°C/350°F/Gas 4.

5 Put the drained quark in a bowl with the egg yolks and caster sugar and mix together. Blend the cornflour in a cup with a little soured cream, then add to the bowl with the remaining soured cream, the lemon rind and juice and vanilla essence. Mix well.

6 Whisk the egg whites in a greaseproof bowl until stiff, then fold into the quark mixture, one-third at a time. Pour the filling into the pastry case and bake for 1–1¼ hours, until golden and firm. Turn off the oven and leave the door ajar. Let the cheesecake cool, then chill for 2 hours.

7 To make the kisel, put the prepared fruit, caster sugar and water into a pan and cook over a low heat until the sugar dissolves and the juices run. Remove the fruit with a slotted spoon and set aside.

8 Blend the arrowroot in a cup with a little cold water, stir into the fruit juices in the pan and bring to the boil, stirring all the time. Return the fruit to the pan and allow to cool, before serving it with the well-chilled cheesecake, decorated with sprigs of mint.

Apple Pancakes

These much-loved pancakes are filled with cinnamon-spiced caramelized apples.

INGREDIENTS

Serves 6
115g/4oz/1 cup plain flour
pinch of salt
2 eggs, beaten
175ml/6fl oz ¾ cup milk
120ml/4fl oz/½ cup water
25g/1oz/2 tbsp butter, melted
sunflower oil, for frying
cinnamon sugar or icing sugar and
    lemon wedges, to serve (optional)

For the filling
75g/3oz/6 tbsp butter
1.5kg/3lb eating apples, cored, peeled
    and sliced
50g/2oz/¼ cup caster sugar
5ml/1 tsp cinnamon

1 Melt the butter for the filling in a heavy-based frying pan. When the foam subsides, add the apple slices. Sprinkle a mixture of the sugar and cinnamon over the apples. Cook, stirring occasionally, until the apples are soft and golden brown. Set aside.

2 Sift the flour and salt into a mixing bowl and make a well in the middle. Add the eggs and gradually mix in the flour.

3 Slowly add the combined milk and the water, beating until smooth. Stir in the melted butter.

4 Heat 10ml/2 tsp oil in a crêpe or small frying pan. Pour in about 30ml/2 tbsp of the batter, tipping the pan to coat the base evenly.

5 Cook the pancake until the underside is golden brown, then turn over and cook the other side. Slide on to a warm plate, cover with foil and set the plate over a pan of simmering water to keep warm. Repeat with the remaining batter mixture, until it is all used up.

6 Divide the apple filling among the pancakes and roll them up. Sprinkle with cinnamon sugar or a dusting of icing sugar, if liked. Serve with lemon wedges to squeeze over.

COOK'S TIP

These pancakes taste equally good filled with sliced pears instead of apples, or a mixture of both apples and pears.

Spicy Apple Cake

Hundreds of German cakes and desserts include this versatile fruit. This moist and spicy *apfelkuchen* can be found on the menu of *Konditoreien*, coffee and tea houses, everywhere.

INGREDIENTS

Serves 12

115g/4oz/1 cup plain flour
115g/4oz/1 cup wholemeal flour
10ml/2 tsp baking powder
5ml/1 tsp cinnamon
2.5ml/½ tsp mixed spice
225g/8oz cooking apple, cored, peeled and chopped
75g/3oz/6 tbsp butter
175g/6oz/generous ¾ cup soft light brown sugar
finely grated rind of 1 small orange
2 eggs, beaten
30ml/2 tbsp milk
whipped cream dusted with cinnamon, to serve

For the topping

4 eating apples, cored and thinly sliced
juice of ½ orange
10ml/2 tsp caster sugar
45ml/3 tbsp apricot jam, warmed and sieved

1 Preheat the oven to 180°C/350°F/ Gas 4. Grease and line a 23cm/9in round loose-bottomed cake tin. Sift the flours, baking powder and spices together in a bowl.

2 Toss the chopped cooking apple in 30ml/2 tbsp of the flour mixture.

3 Cream the butter, brown sugar and orange rind together until light and fluffy. Gradually beat in the eggs, then fold in the flour mixture, the chopped apple and the milk.

4 Spoon the mixture into the cake tin and level the surface.

5 For the topping, toss the apple slices in the orange juice and set them in overlapping circles on top of the cake mixture, pressing down lightly.

6 Sprinkle the caster sugar over the top and bake for 1–1¼ hours, or until risen and firm. Cover with foil if the apples brown too much.

7 Cool in the tin for 10 minutes, then remove to a wire rack. Glaze the apples with the sieved jam. Cut into wedges and serve with whipped cream, sprinkled with cinnamon.

Bavarian Cream

This light dessert is set in a fancy mould and then turned out to serve. Decorate with cream and chocolate leaves or serve simply with fresh fruit.

INGREDIENTS

Serves 6

1 vanilla pod
300ml/½ pint/1¼ cups single cream
15ml/1 tbsp powdered gelatine
45ml/3 tbsp milk
5 egg yolks
50g/2oz/¼ cup caster sugar
300ml/½ pint/1¼ cups double cream
chocolate leaves and a sprinkling of
    cocoa powder, to decorate

COOK'S TIP

If preferred, use 5ml/1 tsp vanilla essence instead of the vanilla pod. Omit Step 1 and whisk the vanilla essence along with the egg yolks and sugar at Step 3.

---

1 Put the vanilla pod and single cream into a small pan. Slowly bring to the boil, then turn off the heat, cover and infuse for 30 minutes. Remove the pod – rinsed well and dried, it can be stored and used again.

2 Sprinkle the gelatine over the milk and leave to soften.

3 Lightly whisk the egg yolks and caster sugar together in a heatproof bowl. Bring the single cream almost to the boil again, then whisk into the egg mixture.

4 Set the bowl over a pan of barely simmering water and cook the custard, stirring, until it thickens enough to coat the back of a wooden spoon. Remove from the heat, add the soaked gelatine and stir until dissolved.

5 Strain the custard into a clean bowl. Cover with a piece of wet greaseproof paper, to prevent a skin forming and leave to cool.

6 Whip the double cream in a bowl until it just holds soft peaks, then fold it into the cooled custard.

7 Rinse individual moulds or a 1.2 litre/2 pint/5 cup ring or fancy mould with water. Pour in the cream mixture and chill for at least 4 hours, or until set.

8 To unmould the Bavarian cream, dip the mould right up to the rim in very hot water for about 5 seconds. Place a serving plate on top, then quickly invert the mould and remove. Decorate with chocolate leaves and a sprinkling of cocoa powder.

Plum Streusel Slices

In Saxony, in eastern Germany, cakes and fruit desserts are frequently made with this crumble or "streusel" topping. Here, plums are used as the filling in this *pflaumenstreusel*.

INGREDIENTS

Makes 14
225g/8oz/1⅓ cups plums, stoned
   and chopped
15ml/1 tbsp lemon juice
50g/2oz/¼ cup sugar
115g/4oz/½ cup butter, softened
50g/2oz/¼ cup caster sugar
1 egg yolk
150g/5oz/1¼ cups plain flour

For the topping
150g/5oz/1¼ cups plain flour
2.5ml/½ tsp baking powder
75g/3oz/6 tbsp butter, chilled
50g/2oz/¼ cup soft light
   brown sugar
50g/2oz/½ cup chopped hazelnuts

1 Preheat the oven to 180°C/350°F/ Gas 4. Grease and base-line a 20cm/8in square cake tin. Put the plums and lemon juice in a small pan and cook over a low heat for 5 minutes, until soft.

2 Add the sugar to the pan and cook gently until dissolved. Simmer for 3–4 minutes until very thick, stirring occasionally. Leave to cool.

3 Beat the butter and caster sugar together in a bowl until light and fluffy. Beat in the egg yolk, then mix in the flour to make a soft dough. Press the mixture into the base of the prepared cake tin. Bake for 15 minutes. Remove from the oven and spoon the cooked plums over the base.

4 Meanwhile, to make the topping, sift the flour and baking powder into a bowl. Rub in the butter until the mixture resembles breadcrumbs. Stir in the sugar and chopped nuts.

5 Sprinkle the topping mixture over the plums and press it down gently. Return the tin to the oven and bake for a further 30 minutes, or until the topping is lightly browned. Leave to cool for 15 minutes, then cut into slices. Remove from the tin when completely cold.

─── COOK'S TIP ───

Fresh apricots are a delicious alternative to plums in this recipe.

Layered Pancake Gâteau

Pancakes in Hungary were originally very basic food: made with only cornflour and water, and then cooked over an open fire. The relative absence of ovens accounts for today's great variety of pancake recipes– both sweet and savoury – in this part of the world. This unusual layered pancake gateau is just one example of this tradition.

INGREDIENTS

Serves 6

5 eggs, separated
50g/2oz/¼ cup caster sugar
175ml/6fl oz/¾ cup milk
50g/2oz/½ cup self-raising flour, sifted
50g/2oz/4 tbsp unsalted butter, melted
175ml/6fl oz/¾ cup soured cream
sifted icing sugar, for dredging
lemon wedges, to serve

For the filling

3 eggs, separated
25g/1oz/¼ cup icing sugar, sifted
grated rind of 1 lemon
2.5ml/½ tsp vanilla sugar
115g/4oz/1 cup ground almonds

1 Preheat the oven to 200°C/400°F/ Gas 6. Grease and line a deep 20–23cm/8–9in springform cake tin. Whisk the egg yolks and caster sugar together in a bowl until thick and creamy, before whisking in the milk.

2 Whisk the egg whites in a grease-free bowl until stiff, then fold into the batter mixture, alternating with spoonfuls of the flour and half the melted butter.

3 Take a frying pan as near to the size of your prepared cake tin as possible, and lightly grease the pan with a little of the remaining melted butter. Tilt to cover the surface.

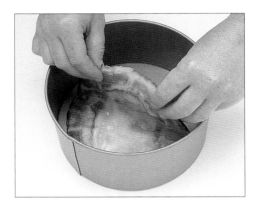

4 Tip one-quarter of the batter into the frying pan. Fry the thick pancake on each side until golden brown, then slide it into the prepared cake tin. Use up the batter to make 3 more pancakes in the same way and set them aside while you make the filling.

5 For the filling, whisk the egg yolks in a bowl with the icing sugar until thick and creamy. Stir in the grated lemon rind and the vanilla sugar.

6 Whisk the egg whites in a separate bowl, then fold them into the egg yolk mixture, before adding the ground almonds. Mix together well.

7 Spread one-third of the mixture on top of the first pancake.

8 Repeat twice more with the second and third pancakes, then top with the final pancake.

9 Spread the soured cream over the top and bake for 20–25 minutes, or until the top is pale golden brown.

10 Leave in the tin for 10 minutes before removing the lining paper. Serve warm, cut into wedges, liberally dusted with icing sugar and accompanied by lemon wedges.

Stewed Fruit

This recipe is good for using up odd or small quantities of fresh fruit. Serve the medley of fruit well chilled.

INGREDIENTS

Serves 6
115–175g/4–6oz/½–¾ cup sugar, depending on the tartness of the fruit
250ml/8fl oz/1 cup cold water
juice and strip of rind from ½ lemon
1 cinnamon stick, broken into two
900g/2lb prepared fruit, such as cored, peeled and sliced apples, pears, quince; stoned plums, peaches, apricots; trimmed gooseberries; cranberries, blueberries, strawberries
30ml/2 tbsp arrowroot
caster sugar and cream (optional), to serve

1 Put the sugar and water into a stainless steel pan and bring to the boil. Add the lemon juice and rind and the two pieces of cinnamon stick. Cook for 1 minute.

2 Add the prepared fruit to the pan and cook for 2–3 minutes only. Remove the fruit and cinnamon stick with a slotted spoon.

3 Blend the arrowroot with a little cold water, stir into the fruit juices and bring to the boil. Return the fruit to the saucepan and allow the fruit to cool before chilling. Discard the cinnamon stick if you wish.

4 Serve the fruit sprinkled with caster sugar, and with whipped cream, if liked.

Sweet Cheese Dumplings

The most famous cheese dumplings come from Czech countries, but they are popular elsewhere, as this Austrian version shows. Sweet and savoury versions combined together, such as this one here, are known as *mehlspeisen*.

INGREDIENTS

Serves 4–6
40g/1½oz/3 tbsp unsalted butter
3 eggs, separated
450g/1lb/2 cups curd cheese
50g/2oz/⅓ cup semolina
15ml/1 tbsp double cream
15–30ml/1–2 tbsp plain flour
sifted icing sugar and sprigs of mint, to decorate

1 Cream the butter and beat in the egg yolks, one at a time. Stir in the curd cheese, semolina and cream. Mix well, cover and stand for 45 minutes.

2 Whisk the egg whites in a grease-free bowl until stiff, then carefully fold into the curd cheese mixture together with the flour.

3 Boil a very large pan of salted water. Scoop spoonfuls of mixture about the size of a plum and roll into ovals or balls with damp hands.

4 Drop the dumplings into the boiling water and simmer for about 6–7 minutes. Remove with a slotted spoon and drain well. Serve warm, dredged liberally with icing sugar and decorated with sprigs of mint.

Nut Squares

This light and delicious Czech recipe is good with coffee in the morning or served as a dessert.

INGREDIENTS

Makes about 24

225g/8oz/1 cup unsalted butter
225g/8oz/generous 1 cup caster sugar
3 egg yolks
175g/6oz/1½ cups plain flour, sifted
4 eggs, beaten
175g/6oz/1½ cups ground walnuts
20g/¾oz/scant ⅓ cup day-old white breadcrumbs
cocoa powder for sprinkling

For the topping

3 egg whites
150g/5oz/¾ cup caster sugar
115g/4oz/1 cup ground walnuts
75g/3oz/½ cup raisins, chopped
25g/1oz/¼ cup cocoa powder, sifted

1 Preheat the oven to 150°C/300°F/ Gas 2. Grease and line a 28 × 18 × 4cm/11 × 7 × 1½ in Swiss roll tin.

2 Cream the butter and caster sugar together until pale and fluffy, then beat in the egg yolks.

3 Fold half the flour into the mixture, then beat in the whole eggs slowly before stirring in the remaining flour and the walnuts.

4 Sprinkle the prepared Swiss roll tin with the breadcrumbs before spooning in the walnut mixture. Level the mixture with a round-bladed knife. Bake for 30–35 minutes or until cooked and pale golden brown.

5 Meanwhile, make the topping. Whisk the egg whites in a grease-free bowl until stiff. Slowly whisk in the sugar until glossy, before folding in the walnuts, raisins and cocoa powder.

6 Spread the topping mixture over the cooked base and cook for a further 15 minutes. Leave to cool in the tin. When cold, peel away the lining paper. Cut into squares or fingers, and sprinkle with cocoa powder.

Lebkuchen

These sweet and spicy cakes, a speciality of Nuremberg in Bavaria, are traditionally baked at Christmas. In German, their name means "cake of life"

INGREDIENTS

Makes 20
115g/4oz/1 cup blanched almonds, finely chopped
50g/2oz/⅓ cup candied orange peel, finely chopped
finely grated rind of ½ lemon
3 cardamom pods
5ml/1 tsp cinnamon
1.5ml/¼ tsp nutmeg
1.5ml/¼ tsp ground cloves
2 eggs
115g/4oz/scant ¾ cup caster sugar
150g/5oz/1¼ cups plain flour
2.5ml/½ tsp baking powder
rice paper (optional)

For the icing
½ egg white
75g/3oz/¾ cup icing sugar, sifted
5ml/1 tsp white rum

1 Preheat the oven to 180°C/350°F/ Gas 4. Set aside some of the almonds for sprinkling and put the remainder in a bowl with the candied orange and lemon rind.

2 Remove the black seeds from the cardamom pods and crush using a pestle and mortar. Add to the bowl with the cinnamon, nutmeg and cloves and mix well.

3 Whisk the eggs and sugar in a mixing bowl until thick and foamy. Sift in the flour and baking powder, then gently fold into the eggs before adding to the nut and spice mixture.

4 Spoon dessertspoons of the mixture on to sheets of rice paper, if using, or baking paper placed on baking sheets, allowing room for the mixture to spread. Sprinkle over the reserved almonds.

5 Bake for 20 minutes, until golden. Allow to cool for a few minutes, then break off the surplus rice paper or remove the biscuits from the baking paper and cool on a wire rack.

6 Put the egg white for the icing in a bowl and lightly whisk with a fork. Stir in a little of the icing sugar at a time, then add the rum. Drizzle over the *lebkuchen* and leave to set. Keep in a tin for 2 weeks before serving.

Stollen

Dating from the 12th century, and symbolizing the Holy Child wrapped in cloth, this traditional German Christmas cake is made from a rich yeast dough with marzipan and dried fruits.

INGREDIENTS

Serves 12

375g/13oz/3 cups strong white
  bread flour
pinch of salt
50g/2oz/¼ cup caster sugar
10ml/2 tsp easy-blend dried yeast
150ml/¼ pint/⅔ cup milk
115g/4oz/½ cup butter
1 egg, beaten
175g/6oz/1 cup mixed
  dried fruit
50g/2oz/¼ cup glacé cherries,
  quartered
50g/2oz/½ cup blanched almonds,
  chopped
finely grated rind of 1 lemon
225g/8oz/1 cup marzipan
icing sugar, for dredging

1 Sift the flour, salt and sugar. Stir in the yeast. Make a well in the centre. Over a low heat, gently melt the milk and butter. Cool, then mix with the egg into the sifted dry ingredients.

2 Turn out the dough on to a lightly floured surface and knead for 10 minutes, until smooth and elastic. Put in a clean bowl, cover with clear film and leave in a warm place to rise for about 1 hour, or until doubled in size.

3 On a lightly floured surface knead in the dried fruit, cherries, almonds and lemon rind.

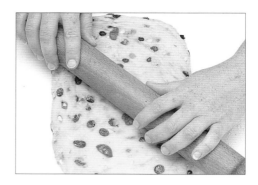

4 Roll out the dough to a rectangle, about 25 × 20cm/10 × 8in.

5 Roll the almond paste to a sausage, slightly shorter than the dough. Place on the dough in the middle. Enclose the paste in dough.

6 Put seam side down on a greased baking sheet. Cover with oiled clear film and leave in a warm place to rise for about 40 minutes, or until doubled in size. Preheat the oven to 190°C/375°F/Gas 5.

7 Bake the stollen for 30–35 minutes, or until golden and hollow sounding when tapped on the underside. Leave to cool on a wire rack. Serve thickly dusted with icing sugar.

Black Bread

Black bread is eaten throughout Eastern Europe. This German yeastless version has a dense texture similar to that of pumpernickel and is steamed rather than oven baked. Empty fruit cans are perfect for producing bread in the traditional round shape.

INGREDIENTS

Makes 2 loaves

50g/2oz/½ cup rye flour
40g/1½ oz/⅓ cup plain flour
4ml/¾ tsp baking powder
2.5ml/½ tsp salt
1.5ml/¼ tsp cinnamon
1.5ml/¼ tsp nutmeg
50g/2oz/⅓ cup fine semolina
60ml/4 tbsp black treacle
200ml/7fl oz/scant 1 cup cultured buttermilk
cherry jam, soured cream or crème fraîche and a sprinkling of ground allspice, to serve

1 Grease and line 2 × 400g/14oz fruit cans. Sift the flours, baking powder, salt and spices into a large bowl. Stir in the semolina.

--- COOK'S TIP ---

If you cannot get buttermilk, use ordinary milk instead, first soured with 5ml/1 tsp lemon juice.

2 Add the black treacle and buttermilk and mix thoroughly.

3 Divide the mixture between the 2 tins, then cover each with a double layer of greased pleated foil.

4 Place the cans on a trivet in a large pan and pour in enough hot water to come halfway up the sides. Cover tightly and steam for 2 hours, checking the water level occasionally.

5 Carefully remove the cans from the steamer. Turn the bread out on to a wire rack and cool completely. Wrap in foil and use within 1 week.

6 Serve the bread in slices, spread with cherry jam, topped with a spoonful of soured cream or crème fraîche and a sprinkling of allspice.

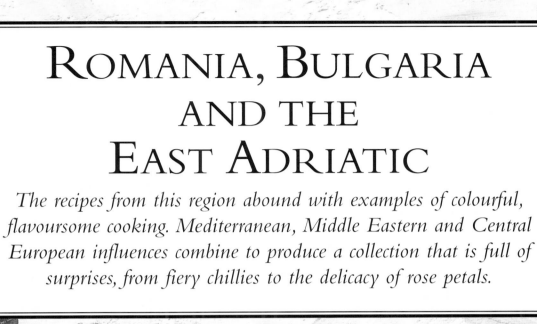

Romania, Bulgaria AND THE East Adriatic

The recipes from this region abound with examples of colourful, flavoursome cooking. Mediterranean, Middle Eastern and Central European influences combine to produce a collection that is full of surprises, from fiery chillies to the delicacy of rose petals.

INTRODUCTION

The southern portion of Eastern Europe lies between the Adriatic and Black Seas, a group of countries commonly referred to as the Balkans. In this fascinating region, the hearty German and Austro-Hungarian cooking styles to the north-west overlap with more exotic culinary traditions borrowed from Turkey and the Near East, plus an occasional Russian influence. The result is a varied cuisine that takes full advantage of the diverse vegetables and herbs grown in the region and tends to be spicier than more northern cooking styles.

QUALITY INGREDIENTS
The accent in all the region's cooking is on flavour and quality. Typical dishes based on everyday ingredients include stuffed cabbage leaves, peppers or aubergines, or raw salad vegetables served with grilled or spit-roasted chicken. Excellent bread, dairy products, fruit, pork and fish also figure prominently in the diet. Wine is being produced in increasing quantities, following ancient traditions as well as new methods.

EXOTIC INFLUENCES
The Turkish influence is most apparent in Romania and Bulgaria, where traditional starters called *meze* include tomatoes, peppers, olives, baked aubergines, bean salads, cheese and ham as well as European sausage. Bulgarian *pasterma*, which is dried beef often combined with paprika, and Dalmatian *prsut*, a dark smoked ham like Italian prosciutto, count among the highlights of the *meze* table. Yogurt, pickled cucumbers, vegetables and such fish delicacies as *tarama* are also popular.

Connoisseurs of Turkish cooking will also recognize the Romanian speciality *placinta* and its Bulgarian and Serbian counterparts. These flaky pastry pies filled with meat or cheese, or cheese and spinach, are usually served hot after *meze*.

FRESH VEGETABLES AND FRUIT
Vegetables are grown in abundance in domestic gardens and allotments and are on sale fresh in markets everywhere. Ranging from all the many northern root crops to the southern summer crops of aubergines, peppers, tomatoes, courgettes and okra, they figure prominently in most dishes. Among the many fruits grown are apricots, peaches and watermelons.

When Bulgarian cooks get to work incorporating vegetables into casseroles, with or without meat, the results are memorable. These oven-baked dishes, called *gyuvech* in Bulgarian, *ghiveci* in Romanian and *djuvec* in Serbian, are named after the earthenware pots in which they are slowly cooked. Bulgarians are also fond of rice dishes, which typically incorporate courgettes or spinach. *Shopska* salad, a typical first course for lunch or dinner in Bulgaria, is made of generous chunks of tomatoes, cucumber and onion dressed with yogurt.

Left: The Balkans and the countries lining the Adriatic Sea, made up of the former Yugoslavia, offer some of the most tasty and surprising food of Eastern Europe. With influences as varied as Turkey and Greece in the south-east, Italy to the west and the rich traditions of the Central European countries, this is hardly surprising.

PRODUCE FROM SEA AND RIVER

Great waterways, including the Danube River, pass through or wash the fringes of the Balkan countries so a strong tradition in fish cookery comes as no surprise. Plates of small fried fish, eaten with chunks of white bread and washed down with wine or cold beer are a delight wherever they are found.

Romania's oldest recipes are for stews and simple grills using the once plentiful river fish of the Danube river and its delta, such as grey mullet and carp, and catfish from the Black Sea. Many of these recipes have been adapted in this book for use with more readily available meaty fish such as tuna, marlin and shark.

Good fish are still abundant along the Dalmatian seaboard of Croatia and Serbia. It is hard to know which to rate higher: a plate of mixed fried fish from the Adriatic or a fish soup with wine and garlic, rosemary and olive oil.

MEAT DISHES

Balkan cooks have excellent ways with meat, whether plain, grilled and served with sour pickles as in Romania, cooked as kebabs or casseroled with vegetables in the Bulgarian style.

Romanians and Croatians also specialize in delicious, barbecued, spicy meatballs of pork or mixed pork and beef served with peppers preserved in olive oil.

Pork and fried chips is an easily prepared but reliable dish found everywhere, although with a little more effort the meat may be simmered in beer. Pork fat is widely used for cooking in Romania, where a family living on the edge of a small town might well keep a pig for its own use.

Lamb is most popular in Bulgaria, where it is usually grilled or cubed in a casserole.

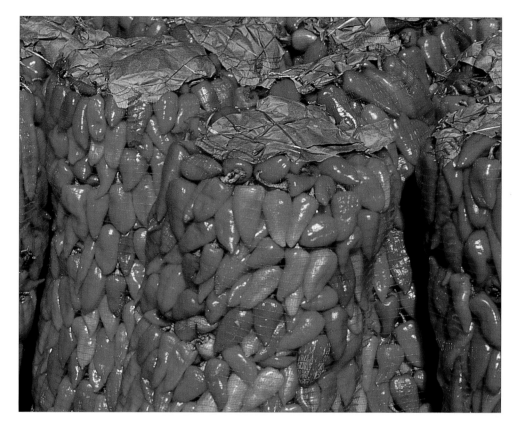

Above: Sacks of fresh red chillies ready for sale in a Serbian market. Peppers are used both fresh and pickled.

SOUPS

Many foreigners asked to nominate their favourite Balkan dish might elect bean soup. While all East European countries have their individual recipes for bean soup, it is the addition of hot and sour elements by Romanian and Bulgarian cooks that earns their soups a first prize for texture and sheer gutsy flavour. The distinctive sour tang is usually provided by lemon juice but can also be from vinegar, bitter fruits or pickles.

Tarator, an unusual cold soup made with cucumber, yogurt and walnuts, is a delicious example of some of the region's excellent and refreshing summer cooking.

DESSERTS

A sweet course in Romania might be a cherry strudel, a sweet jam- or fruit-filled pancake reminiscent of an Austrian favourite. The classic Bulgarian dessert, usually a creamy rice pudding, is flavoured with rose water. In Slovenia it might be a rich, sweet, boiled pudding, almost Anglo-Saxon in style, such as *potica*, which may be made using buckwheat flour and chestnuts.

Chestnuts, walnuts and other nuts such as pistachios are widely used in sweet bakery. They make an appearance in French-inspired tarts as well as in Eastern-style cakes that drip syrup, as typified by *baklava*.

Any Balkan meal might end with a Turkish-style coffee, served with what the Romanians call a *dulceata* and the Serbians a *slatko*. These sweetmeats consist of either Turkish delight or soft sweets made from apples, plums, raisins, sultanas or figs, which have been stewed, thickened and rolled into balls, before perhaps being coated with nuts. They may be dipped in rum or other alcohol.

INGREDIENTS

Left, from front: tomatoes, capsicum, large fresh chillies, aubergines, courgettes, cucumber and beans.

Below, from the back: salmon, grey mullet, octopus, sea bass, mackerel, whitebait and trout.

VEGETABLES
Southern vegetables such as peppers, aubergines, courgettes and tomatoes all feature strongly in Balkan cuisine, together with more northerly onions and cabbage. Piquant stews of peppers and aubergines with garlic, vinegar and oil are used as relishes or cooked salads served with bread. Romanian grilled meat dishes are often accompanied by pickled vegetables, such as cucumbers or chillies.

FISH
The predominant inland fish, that might once have been caught in the Danube, are carp, grey mullet, river trout, sturgeon and sterlet, pike, perch, bream and freshwater crayfish. Traditionally, excellent catfish comes from the Danube delta, while on the Adriatic coast squid and octopus are caught, as well as mackerel, sardines, tuna and white fish such as sea bass and gilt-head bream. Species found in the Black Sea include grey mullet and scad, small oily fish which resemble whitebait and are fried in batter and eaten whole.

DAIRY PRODUCTS
Kashkaval, properly made from ewe's milk, is the general name for the yellow cheese produced in the Balkans. Depending on how it is made it can be piquant, or rubbery and bland. It is often available from Greek, Middle Eastern and Cypriot delicatessens and is excellent for grating, toasting and frying. A good substitute is Italian pecorino. *Brinza* is the Romanian equivalent of the brine cheese used throughout East European cooking, for which feta may be substituted.

Bulgarian yogurt has become a legendary source of health and longevity, but it may be replaced by any good quality live organic yogurt. It is the key ingredient in a cold cucumber soup of the region. A unique Serbian speciality is *kaimak*, which is thick cream made from boiled milk.

Far left, clockwise from left: red kidney beans, mamaliga, haricot beans and black kidney beans.

Left, clockwise from left: peaches, lemons, oranges, apricots, cherries, pistachios and shelled walnuts.

GRAINS AND PULSES

Mamaliga, cooked cornmeal used as a staple accompaniment to meat dishes, or with cheese or bacon, is a distinctive Romanian speciality, although it is now encountered less often than it was 50 years ago. The tradition of making this bright yellow porridge came to Europe from the New World in the 16th century, and it has remained a favourite also with the Italians, who call it polenta.

The handground cornmeal was cooked in water over an open fire until it was so thick that it could be sliced like bread when cool. The tools for making *mamaliga*, an iron cauldron and a large wooden stirring stick, are prized decorative objects.

Red and black kidney beans and white haricot or lima beans are widely used in soups.

FRUIT AND NUTS

Cherries, peaches, apricots, figs and watermelons are widely enjoyed when in season. Chestnuts form an important part of sweet baking in some regions such as Slovenia, as do apples, and Balkan pastries of all kinds are filled with the walnuts and hazelnuts that grow in abundance. Walnuts are also used to thicken the typical cold soups.

HERBS, SPICES AND OTHER FLAVOURINGS

Fresh herbs such as parsley, thyme, tarragon, basil, savory, mint and dill are widely used in the Balkans – in salads, soups and casseroles. Chilli peppers give a typical fire to Balkan cooking. A more unusual herb, lovage, comparable with the taste of celery leaves, is typically used in Romanian cooking, especially in lamb soup. It is not difficult to buy and is also easily grown at home. The Balkan countries also have a taste for soups soured with lemon juice or a dash of vinegar.

Rose water and rose petals flavour and decorate Bulgarian desserts, such as rice puddings. The Valley of the Roses, which crosses Bulgaria from west to east, was planted by the Turks in the 17th century; since then, it has become the home of the precious oil called rose attar, and the basis of a small industry in soap and rose liqueur.

Right, clockwise from front left: fresh chillies, vinegar, olive oil, fresh herbs, rose water and petals, dried thyme, Kashkaval ewe's milk cheese, yogurt and olives (centre).

DRINKS

Coffee of the strong, thick Turkish variety is widely loved throughout the Balkans and east Adriatic countries. It is often served with an accompanying sweetmeat such as *lokum* (Turkish delight).

Maraschino, made of cherries, *travarica*, flavoured with herbs, and *slivovica* (slivowicz), a plum brandy, are all popular liqueurs in the countries of the former Yugoslavia. The Romanian national spirit is *tuica*, a very potent plum eau de vie or brandy. Bulgaria produces a rose liqueur and also one of aniseed, called *mastica*, which is similar to the Greek raki.

SOUPS AND STARTERS

East Europeans are renowned for their hospitality, and home-made soup is often to be found on the stove, ready for eating at any time of the day. Sour-flavoured soups, called chorbas, are a traditional speciality of this region, as is the unusual combination of fruit and vegetables in their soups.
Meze, or starters, reflect the typical flavours and ingredients of the region, such as local cheeses, fresh fish and seafood, tomatoes, capsicums and herbs and spices. Served hot or cold, they are the perfect beginning to a meal.

Cold Cucumber and Yogurt Soup with Walnuts

A refreshing cold soup, using a classic combination of cucumber and yogurt, typical of the area.

INGREDIENTS

Serves 5–6
1 cucumber
4 garlic cloves
2.5ml/½ tsp salt
75g/3oz/¾ cup walnut pieces
40g/1½ oz day-old bread, torn
   into pieces
30ml/2 tbsp walnut or sunflower oil
400ml/14fl oz/1²⁄₃ cups cow's or
   sheep's yogurt
120ml/4fl oz/½ cup cold water or
   chilled still mineral water
5–10ml/1–2 tsp lemon juice

For the garnish
40g/1½ oz/scant ½ cup walnuts,
   coarsely chopped
25ml/1½ tbsp olive oil
sprigs of fresh dill

1 Cut the cucumber into 2 and peel one half of it. Dice the cucumber flesh and set aside.

2 Using a large mortar and pestle, crush the garlic and salt together well; add the walnuts and bread.

COOK'S TIP

If you prefer your soup smooth, purée it in a food processor or blender before serving.

3 When the mixture is smooth, add the walnut or sunflower oil slowly and combine well.

4 Transfer the mixture into a large bowl and beat in the yogurt and diced cucumber.

5 Add the cold water or mineral water and lemon juice to taste.

6 Pour the soup into chilled soup bowls to serve. Garnish with the coarsely chopped walnuts, a little olive oil drizzled over the nuts and sprigs of fresh dill.

Bulgarian Sour Lamb Soup

This soup – a variation on the basic traditional sour soup, or *chorba* – has long been associated with Bulgaria. This recipe uses lamb, though pork or poultry are also popular.

INGREDIENTS

Serves 4–5
30ml/2 tbsp oil
450g/1lb lean lamb, trimmed
   and cubed
1 onion, diced
30ml/2 tbsp plain flour
15ml/1 tbsp paprika
1 litre/1¾ pints/4 cups hot lamb stock
3 parsley sprigs
4 spring onions
4 dill sprigs
25g/1oz/scant ¼ cup long-grain rice
2 eggs, beaten
30–45ml/2–3 tbsp or more vinegar
   or lemon juice
salt and freshly ground black pepper
crusty bread, to serve

For the garnish
25g/1oz/2 tbsp butter, melted
5ml/1 tsp paprika
a little parsley or lovage and dill

1 In a large pan heat the oil and then brown the meat. Add the onion and cook until it has softened.

2 Sprinkle in the flour and paprika. Stir well, add the stock and cook for 10 minutes.

3 Tie the parsley, spring onions and dill together with string and add to the pan with the rice and a little salt and pepper. Bring to the boil then simmer for about 30–40 minutes, or until the lamb is tender.

COOK'S TIP

Do not reheat this soup since the eggs could become scrambled.

4 Remove the pan from the heat then add the beaten eggs, stirring continuously. Add the vinegar or lemon juice. Remove and discard the tied herbs and season to taste.

5 For the garnish, melt the butter and paprika together in a small pan. Ladle the soup into warmed serving bowls. Garnish with herbs and a little red paprika butter. Serve with thick chunks of bread.

Apple Soup

Romania has vast fruit orchards, and this soup is a delicious result of that natural resource.

INGREDIENTS

Serves 6
1 kohlrabi
3 carrots
2 celery sticks
1 green pepper, seeded
2 tomatoes
45ml/3 tbsp oil
2 litres/3½ pints/8 cups
   chicken stock
6 large green apples
45ml/3 tbsp plain flour
150ml/¼ pint/⅔ cup double cream
15ml/1 tbsp granulated sugar
30–45ml/2–3 tbsp lemon juice
salt and freshly ground black pepper
lemon wedges and crusty bread,
   to serve

1 Dice the kohlrabi, carrots, celery, green pepper and tomatoes in a large pan, add the oil and fry for 5–6 minutes until just softened.

2 Pour in the chicken stock, bring to the boil then reduce the heat and simmer for 45 minutes.

3 Meanwhile, peel, core and dice the apples, then add to the pan and simmer for a further 15 minutes.

4 In a bowl, mix together the flour and double cream then pour slowly into the soup, stirring well, and bring to the boil. Add the sugar and lemon juice before seasoning to taste. Serve immediately accompanied by lemon wedges and crusty bread.

Chick-pea Soup

Chick-peas form part of the staple diet in the Balkans, used either whole or ground. This soup is economical to make, and various spicy sausages may be added to give extra flavour.

INGREDIENTS

Serves 4–6
500g/1¼lb/3½ cups chick-peas,
   rinsed and drained well
2 litres/3½ pints/8 cups chicken or
   vegetable stock
3 large waxy potatoes, peeled and cut
   into bite-size chunks
50ml/2fl oz/¼ cup olive oil
225g/8oz spinach leaves, washed and
   drained well
salt and freshly ground black pepper

1 Place the chick-peas in a bowl of cold water and leave overnight. The next day, drain them well and place in a large pan with the stock.

2 Bring to the boil, then reduce the heat and cook gently for about 55 minutes. Add the potatoes, olive oil and seasoning, and cook for 20 minutes.

3 Five minutes before the end of cooking, add the spinach. Serve the soup in warmed soup bowls.

Lamb Meatball Soup with Vegetables

This family recipe is an ideal way to use up leftover vegetables.

INGREDIENTS

Serves 4

1 litre/1³/₄ pints/4 cups lamb stock
1 onion, finely chopped
2 carrots, finely sliced
¹/₂ celeriac, finely diced
75g/3oz/³/₄ cup frozen peas
50g/2oz green beans, cut into
    2.5cm/1in pieces
3 tomatoes, seeded and chopped
1 red pepper, seeded and finely diced
1 potato, coarsely diced
2 lemons, sliced
salt and freshly ground black pepper
crusty bread, to serve

For the meatballs

225g/8oz very lean minced lamb
40g/1¹/₂oz/¹/₄ cup short-grain rice
30ml/2 tbsp chopped fresh parsley
plain flour, for coating
salt and freshly ground black pepper

1 Put the stock, all of the vegetables, the slices of lemon and a little seasoning in a large pan. Bring to the boil, then reduce the heat and simmer for 15–20 minutes.

2 Meanwhile, for the meatballs, combine the minced meat, rice and parsley together in a bowl and season well.

3 Roll the mixture into small balls, roughly the size of walnuts and toss them in the flour.

4 Drop the meatballs into the soup and simmer gently for 25–30 minutes, stirring occasionally, to prevent the meatballs from sticking. Adjust the seasoning to taste and serve the soup in warmed serving bowls, accompanied by crusty bread.

Fried Peppers with Cheese

This traditional Bulgarian dish may vary slightly from place to place in the Balkan area, but it is usually served as a starter or light snack. The peppers may be red, yellow or green.

INGREDIENTS

Serves 2–4
4 long peppers
50g/2oz/½ cup plain flour, seasoned
1 egg, beaten
olive oil, for shallow frying
cucumber and tomato salad,
    to serve

For the filling
1 egg, beaten
90g/3½ oz/scant ½ cup feta cheese,
    finely crumbled
30ml/2 tbsp chopped fresh parsley
1 small chilli, seeded and
    finely chopped

1 Slit open the peppers lengthways, enabling you to scoop out the seeds and remove the cores, but leaving the peppers in one piece.

2 Carefully open out the peppers and place under a preheated grill, skin side uppermost. Cook until the skin is charred and blackened. Place the peppers on a plate, cover with clear film and leave for 10 minutes.

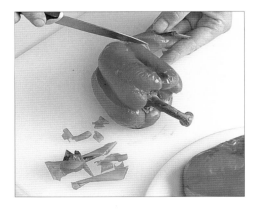

3 Using a sharp knife, carefully peel away the skin from the peppers.

4 In a bowl mix together well all the filling ingredients. Divide evenly among the four peppers.

5 Reshape the peppers to look whole. Dip them into the seasoned flour, then the egg then the flour again.

6 Fry the peppers gently in a little olive oil for 6–8 minutes, turning once, or until golden brown and the filling is set. Drain the peppers on kitchen paper before serving with a cucumber and tomato salad.

Bessarabian Pancakes

Bessarabia is the historical name for modern Moldova, in Romania, the source for this spinach and cheese pancake.

INGREDIENTS

Serves 4–6
4 eggs, beaten
40g/1½oz/3tbsp butter, melted
250ml/8fl oz/1 cup single cream
250ml/8fl oz/1 cup soda water
175g/6oz/1½ cups plain flour, sifted
pinch of salt
1 egg white, lightly beaten
oil, for frying

For the filling
350g/12oz/1½ cups feta cheese, crumbled
50g/2oz/⅔ cup Parmesan cheese, grated
40g/1½oz/3 tbsp butter
1 garlic clove, crushed
450g/1lb frozen spinach, thawed
shavings of Parmesan, to garnish

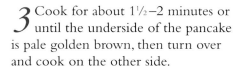

1 Blend the eggs, butter, cream and water in a food processor or blender. With the motor running, spoon in the flour and salt through the feeder tube until the batter mixture is smooth and lump free. Leave to stand for 15 minutes to rest, loosely covered with clear film.

2 Lightly grease a 13–15cm/5–6in non-stick frying pan and place over a medium heat. When hot, pour in 45–60ml/3–4 tbsp of the batter, tilting the pan to spread the mixture thinly.

3 Cook for about 1½–2 minutes or until the underside of the pancake is pale golden brown, then turn over and cook on the other side.

4 Repeat the process until all the batter has been used, stacking the pancakes on a warm plate as you go.

5 For the filling, in a clean bowl mix together well the crumbled feta and Parmesan cheese, the butter and garlic clove. Thoroughly stir in the squeeze-dried spinach.

6 Place 30–45ml/2–3 tbsp of the filling mixture on to the centre of each pancake. Brush a little egg white around the outer edges of the pancakes and then fold them over. Press the edges down well to seal.

7 Fry the pancakes in a little oil on both sides, turning gently, until they are golden brown and the filling is hot. Serve immediately, garnished with Parmesan shavings.

Cheese Scrolls

These delicious Bulgarian cheese savouries are traditionally served warm as a first course, or else as a snack in cafés, restaurants and homes at any time of the day.

INGREDIENTS

Makes 14–16
450g/1lb/2 cups feta cheese, well drained and finely crumbled
90ml/6 tbsp natural Greek yogurt
2 eggs, beaten
14–16 sheets 40 × 30cm/16 × 12in ready-made filo pastry, thawed if frozen
225g/8oz/1 cup unsalted butter, melted
sea salt and chopped spring onions, to garnish

1 Preheat the oven to 200°C/400°F/ Gas 6. In a large bowl mix together the feta cheese, yogurt and eggs, beating well until the mixture is smooth.

2 Fit a piping bag with a large 1cm/ ½in plain round nozzle and fill with half of the cheese mixture.

— COOK'S TIP —

If possible, use the locally made sheep's cheese, *bryndza*. Made throughout Eastern Europe, it is a subtly flavoured, crumbly and moist cheese that resembles feta, but it is not as salty. It is increasingly available in Middle Eastern or Cypriot delicatessens.

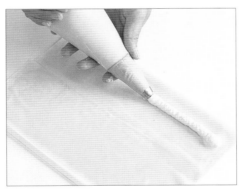

3 Lay out one sheet of pastry, fold into a 30 × 20cm/12 × 8in rectangle and brush with a little melted butter. Along one long edge pipe the cheese mixture 5mm/¼in away from the edge.

4 Roll up the pastry to form a sausage shape and tuck in each end, to prevent the filling escaping. Brush with more melted butter.

5 Form the "sausage" into a tight "S" or a crescent shape. Repeat with the remaining ingredients, refilling the piping bag as necessary.

6 Arrange the scrolls on a buttered baking sheet and sprinkle with a little sea salt and chopped spring onion. Bake for 20 minutes, or until golden brown and crispy. Cool on a wire rack, before serving.

Aubergine and Pepper Spread

This spread is typical of rich, cooked vegetable mixtures, which can be used on breads, as a dip or with grilled meat.

Ingredients

Serves 6–8
675g/1½lb aubergines,
   halved lengthways
2 green peppers, seeded and quartered
45ml/3 tbsp olive oil
2 firm ripe tomatoes, halved, seeded
   and finely chopped
45ml/3 tbsp chopped fresh parsley
   or coriander
2 garlic cloves, crushed
30ml/2 tbsp red wine vinegar
lemon juice, to taste
salt and freshly ground black pepper
sprigs of parsley or coriander,
   to garnish
dark rye bread and lemon wedges,
   to serve

1 Place the aubergines and peppers under a preheated grill, skin side uppermost, and cook until the skin blisters and chars. Turn the vegetables over and cook for a further 3 minutes. Place in a polythene bag and leave for 10 minutes.

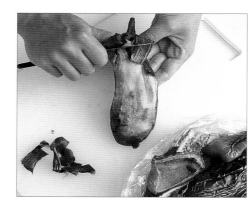

2 Peel away the blackened skin and purée the aubergine and pepper flesh in a food processor.

3 With the motor running, pour the olive oil in a continuous stream, through the feeder tube.

4 Carefully remove the blade and stir in the chopped tomatoes, parsley or coriander, garlic, vinegar and lemon juice. Season to taste, garnish with fresh parsley or coriander and serve with dark rye bread and wedges of lemon.

Tarama

This well-known hors d'oeuvre is made from hard fish roes, generally from grey mullet or cod, to which salt has been added as a preservative.

Ingredients

Serves 4–6
115g/4oz/8 tbsp smoked tarama or
   cod's roe
15ml/1 tbsp lemon juice
175ml/6fl oz/¾ cup olive oil, plus a
   little extra for drizzling
20g/¾oz finely grated onion
15–25ml/1–1½ tbsp boiling water
paprika, for sprinkling
black olives and celery leaves,
   to garnish
toast, to serve

1 Soak the cod's roe in cold water for 2 hours. Drain, then peel off any outer skin and membrane from the roe and discard it. Process the roe in a food processor or blender at a low speed.

2 Add the lemon juice and then, with the motor still running, slowly add the olive oil through the feeder tube.

3 Once thickened, beat in the onion and water. Spoon into a serving bowl and chill well. Sprinkle with a little paprika. Garnish with the olives and celery leaves. Drizzle with a little oil and serve with toasted bread.

Grilled Pepper Salad

This Romanian dish, *Salata de Ardei*, is generally served as a starter (*meze*), or as a dish to accompany cold meats. *Meze* are served on a flat dish divided into different sections so that another three or four complementary *meze* may be added, such as diced salami, feta cheese, olives or pickle.

INGREDIENTS

Serves 4

8 long green and/or orange peppers
1 garlic clove, crushed
75ml/5 tbsp olive oil
60ml/4 tbsp wine vinegar
4 tomatoes, sliced
1 red onion, thinly sliced
freshly ground black pepper
sprigs of fresh coriander,
    to garnish
black bread, to serve

1 Cut the peppers into quarters, discarding the cores, seeds and tops. Place under a preheated grill, skin side uppermost, and cook until the skin chars and blisters.

— COOK'S TIP —

The long peppers used in this recipe are increasingly available, but if you cannot find them use small ordinary peppers.

2 Place the peppers in a polythene bag and leave for 15 minutes.

3 Remove the peppers from the bag and scrape off the skins using a sharp knife.

4 Blend together the garlic, olive oil and vinegar. Arrange the peppers, tomatoes and onion on four serving plates and pour over the garlic dressing. Season, garnish with sprigs of coriander and serve with black bread.

Octopus Salad

The Adriatic Sea separates Italy and the former Yugoslavian countries, which accounts for many of the similarities between their cuisines – particularly in their fondness for fresh fish and seafood, olives, oil and vinegar.

INGREDIENTS

Serves 4–6

900g/2lb baby octopus or squid, skinned
175ml/6fl oz/³⁄₄ cup olive oil
30ml/2 tbsp white wine vinegar
30ml/2 tbsp chopped fresh parsley or coriander
12 black olives, stoned
2 shallots, thinly sliced
1 red onion, thinly sliced
salt and freshly ground black pepper
sprigs of coriander, to garnish
8–12 cos lettuce leaves and lemon wedges, to serve

1 In a large saucepan, boil the octopus or squid in salted water for 20–25 minutes, or until just soft. Strain and leave to cool before covering and chilling for 45 minutes.

COOK'S TIP

Take care not to overcook the octopus or squid or it will become tough and rubbery.

2 Cut the tentacles from the body and head, then chop all the flesh into even pieces, slicing across the thick part of the tentacles following the direction of the suckers.

3 In a bowl, combine the olive oil and white wine vinegar.

4 Add the parsley, olives, shallots, octopus and red onion to the bowl. Season to taste and toss well.

5 Arrange the octopus on a bed of lettuce, garnish with coriander and serve with lemon wedges.

MEAT AND POULTRY

Lamb has long reigned supreme throughout the Balkans, and it has resulted in many delicious dishes, such as the classic kebab and slowly cooked casseroles and stews, and pastry-encased whole joints for special occasions.

Balkan cooking has been shaped by many influences, producing a surprising variety. The recipe for Pork Schnitzel, combining sour cream with pork, is reminiscent of its northern neighbours Hungary and Austria, and the addition of spices to Rolled Beef gives that dish a distinctive Turkish flavour.

Lamb-stuffed Squash

This recipe is ideal for using any leftover cooked meat and rice.

INGREDIENTS

Serves 6 as a main course, 12 as a starter
6 acorn squash, halved
45ml/3tbsp lemon juice
25g/1oz/2 tbsp butter
30ml/2 tbsp plain flour
250ml/8fl oz/1 cup whipping cream
175ml/6fl oz/³/₄ cup passata
115g/4oz/¹/₂ cup feta cheese, crumbled
  and basil leaves, to garnish, plus
  extra, to serve

For the filling
350–450g/12–16oz cooked lean lamb
175g/6oz cooked long-grain rice
25g/1oz/2 tbsp butter, melted
25g/1oz/¹/₂ cup fresh breadcrumbs
50ml/2fl oz/¹/₄ cup milk
30ml/2 tbsp finely grated onion
30ml/2 tbsp chopped fresh parsley
2 eggs, beaten
salt and freshly ground black pepper

1 Preheat the oven to 180°C/350°F/ Gas 4. Trim the bases of the squash, if necessary, so that they will stand up securely. Using a teaspoon, remove the insides of the squash, taking care not to cut the outer skin or base. Leave about 1cm/¹/₂in of flesh from the base.

2 Blanch the squash in boiling water with the lemon juice for 2–3 minutes, then plunge them into cold water. Drain well and leave to cool.

3 Meanwhile, make the filling by combining in a bowl the cooked lamb and rice, the butter, breadcrumbs, milk, onion, parsley, eggs and seasoning. Place the squash in a lightly greased ovenproof dish, and fill with the lamb mixture.

4 To make the sauce, put the butter and flour in a pan. Whisk in the cream and bring to the boil, whisking all the time. Cook for 1–2 minutes until thickened, then season well. Pour the sauce over the prepared squash, then pour over the passata.

5 Bake the squash in the oven for 25–30 minutes. Drizzle them with a little of the sauce, and sprinkle with feta cheese and basil leaves. Serve separately any extra sauce, feta and basil.

---— COOK'S TIP —---

You could use a thick courgette or a marrow instead of the squash, removing the seeds in the same way.

Bulgarian Lamb in Pastry

This is an impressive dish to serve on special occasions. Skim the meat juices, bring them back to the boil and serve as a gravy with the lamb.

INGREDIENTS

Serves 6–8

1.5kg/3½lb leg of lamb, boned
40g/1½oz/3 tbsp butter
2.5ml/½ tsp each dried thyme, basil and oregano
2 garlic cloves, crushed
45ml/3tbsp lemon juice
salt, for sprinkling
1 egg, beaten, for sealing and glazing
1 oregano or marjoram sprig, to garnish

For the pastry

450g/1lb/4 cups plain flour, sifted
250g/9oz/generous 1 cup chilled butter, diced
150–250ml/¼–½ pint/²⁄₃–1 cup iced water

1 Preheat the oven to 190°/375°F/ Gas 5. To make the pastry, place the flour and butter into a food processor or blender and process until the mixture resembles fine breadcrumbs. Add enough iced water to make a soft, but not sticky, dough. Knead gently and form into a ball. Wrap in clear film and refrigerate for 1–2 hours.

2 Meanwhile, put the lamb in a roasting tin, tie the joint with string and cut 20 small holes in the meat, with a sharp, narrow knife.

3 Cream together the butter, dried herbs, garlic and lemon juice and use to fill the small cuts in the lamb. Sprinkle the whole joint with salt.

4 Cook the lamb in a roasting tin for about 1 hour, then allow to cool. Remove the string.

5 Roll out the pastry on a lightly floured surface until large enough to wrap around the lamb in one piece. Seal the pastry edges with a little of the egg and place in a clean tin.

6 With any remaining scraps of pastry make leaves or other shapes to decorate the pastry. Brush with more of the egg. Return to the oven and bake for a further 30–45 minutes. Serve hot, in slices, accompanied by the gravy from the meat juices, and garnished with a sprig of oregano or marjoram.

Meat Loaf

Like many Serbian recipes, this dish is easy to make, requiring nothing more than good quality meat and plenty of fresh herbs.

INGREDIENTS

Serves 4–6
8 smoked streaky, rindless
  bacon rashers
2 lean bacon rashers, diced
1 onion, finely chopped
2 garlic cloves, crushed
115g/4oz/2 cups fresh breadcrumbs
90ml/6 tbsp milk
450g/1lb lean minced beef
450g/1lb lean minced pork
2.5ml/½ tsp chopped fresh thyme
30ml/2 tbsp chopped fresh parsley
2 eggs, beaten
salt and freshly ground black pepper
herby mashed potatoes and carrots,
  to serve

1 Preheat the oven to 200°C/400°F/ Gas 6. Line a 1.75 litre/3 pint/ 7½ cup buttered loaf tin with the rashers of streaky bacon. Stretch the rashers with the back of a knife, if necessary, to completely fill the tin.

2 Dry fry the diced bacon in a large frying pan until almost crisp. Stir in the onion and garlic and fry for a further 2–3 minutes until they are soft and a pale golden brown.

3 In a large bowl soak the bread-crumbs in the milk for 5 minutes, or until all the milk is absorbed.

4 Add the minced meats, bacon, onion, garlic, herbs and eggs to the breadcrumbs. Season and mix well.

5 Spoon the mixture into the loaf tin. Level the top and cover the tin with foil. Bake for about 1½ hours. Turn out and serve in slices, with herby mashed potatoes and carrots.

Pork with Sauerkraut

The presence of sauerkraut and mustard suggests links with Central European cuisines, but the presence of chillies is a purely southern touch.

INGREDIENTS

Serves 4
450g/1lb lean pork or veal, diced
60ml/4 tbsp vegetable oil or
  melted lard
2.5ml/½ tsp paprika
400g/14oz shredded sauerkraut,
  drained and well rinsed
2 fresh red chillies
90ml/6 tbsp pork stock
salt and freshly ground black pepper
50ml/2fl oz/¼ cup soured cream
coarse grain mustard, paprika and sage
  leaves, to garnish
crusty bread, to serve

1 In a heavy-based frying pan cook the pork or veal in the oil until browned on all sides.

2 Add the paprika and shredded sauerkraut. Stir well and transfer to a flameproof casserole.

3 Halve the chillies and remove the seeds before burying the chillies in the middle of the casserole.

4 Add the stock to the casserole. Cover tightly and cook over a gentle heat for 1–1½ hours, stirring occasionally to prevent it sticking.

5 Remove the chillies, if liked, and season to taste before serving. Spoon on the soured cream and spoonfuls of mustard, sprinkle with paprika and garnish with sage leaves. Serve with crusty bread.

Pork Schnitzel

This Croatian recipe features Central European ingredients.

INGREDIENTS

Serves 4
4 pork leg steaks or escalopes, about 200g/7oz each
60ml/4 tbsp olive oil
115g/4oz chicken livers, chopped
1 garlic clove, crushed
plain flour, seasoned, for coating
salt and freshly ground black pepper
15ml/1 tbsp chopped fresh parsley to garnish

For the sauce

1 onion, thinly sliced
115g/4oz streaky bacon, thinly sliced
175g/6oz/ 2 cups mixed wild mushrooms, sliced
120ml/4fl oz/½ cup olive oil
5ml/1 tsp ready-made mustard
150ml/¼ pint/⅔ cup white wine
120ml/4fl oz/½ cup soured cream
250ml/8fl oz/1 cup double cream
salt and freshly ground black pepper

1 Place the pork between 2 sheets of dampened polythene, clear film or greaseproof paper and flatten with a meat mallet or rolling pin until about 15 × 10cm/6 × 4in. Season well.

2 Heat half the oil in a frying pan and cook the chicken livers and garlic for 1–2 minutes. Remove, drain on kitchen paper and leave to cool.

— COOK'S TIP —

If liked, replace the pork with veal or chicken and cook in the same way.

3 Divide the livers evenly between the four prepared pork steaks and roll up into neat parcels. Secure with cocktail sticks or string before rolling lightly in the seasoned flour.

4 Heat the remaining oil and gently fry the schnitzels for 6–8 minutes on each side, or until golden brown. Drain on kitchen paper and keep warm.

5 Meanwhile, to make the sauce, fry the onion, bacon and mushrooms in the oil for 2–3 minutes, then add the mustard, white wine and soured cream. Stir to simmering point, then add the double cream and season.

6 Arrange the schnitzels on plates with a little of the sauce spooned around and the rest poured into a serving jug. Garnish with the parsley.

Spicy Rolled Beef

This recipe is a blend of Slovakian, Greek and Russian cuisines, with a spicy touch of coriander and peppercorns.

INGREDIENTS

Serves 4

4 thick 10–15cm/4–6in beef slices
50ml/2fl oz/¼ cup olive or vegetable
    oil, plus extra for frying
30ml/2 tbsp black peppercorns,
    roughly crushed
30ml/2 tbsp whole coriander seeds
1 onion, finely sliced
300ml/½ pint/1¼ cups Bulgarian
    or dry red wine
1 egg, beaten
150g/5oz can chopped tomatoes
polenta and soured cream, to serve

For the filling

115g/4oz/½ cup minced ham
40g/1½oz/scant 1 cup breadcrumbs
2 spring onions, finely sliced
45ml/3 tbsp chopped fresh parsley
1 egg yolk
75g/3oz green pepper, seeded and
    finely chopped
1.5ml/¼ tsp ground allspice

1 Place the slices of beef between 2 sheets of dampened polythene, clear film or greaseproof paper. Flatten with a meat mallet or rolling pin until the meat is evenly thin. Dip the slices in the oil.

2 Lay the meat out flat and sprinkle over the crushed peppercorns, coriander seeds and onion.

3 Roll up the meat neatly and place in a shallow glass or china dish. Pour over half of the wine, cover with clear film and chill for 2 hours.

4 Meanwhile, combine all the filling ingredients together in a bowl and add a little water or beef stock if necessary, to moisten the stuffing.

5 Remove the beef from the bowl and shake off the spices and onion. Spoon 30–45ml/2–3 tbsp of the filling into the middle of each piece of meat.

6 Brush the inner surface with egg and roll up well. Secure with a cocktail stick or tie with string.

7 Heat a little oil in a frying pan and sauté the rolls until brown on all sides. Reduce the heat and pour over the remaining wine and canned tomatoes. Simmer for 25–30 minutes, or until the meat is tender. Season well and serve the beef with the sauce, the polenta and soured cream and plenty of cracked pepper. Garnish with a sprig of parsley.

Veal Escalopes

This simple dish is based on a German recipe, with the noodles adding a touch of the Mediterannean.

INGREDIENTS

Serves 4
4 veal escalopes, about 175g/6oz each
75g/3oz/²/₃ cup plain flour, seasoned
2 eggs, beaten
115g/4oz/scant 2 cups dried
    breadcrumbs
30ml/2 tbsp oil
50g/2oz/4 tbsp butter
coarsely ground white pepper
vegetable oil, for brushing
chives and paprika, to garnish
lemon wedges, buttered tagliatelle and
    green salad, to serve

1 Place the veal escalopes in between 2 sheets of dampened polythene, clear film or greaseproof paper and flatten with a meat mallet or rolling pin until half as large again. Press a little ground white pepper into both sides of the escalopes.

2 Tip the flour, eggs and breadcrumbs on to separate plates. Brush the meat with a little oil then dip into the flour. Shake off any extra flour. Then dip the escalopes into the egg and then finally the breadcrumbs. Leave, loosely covered, for 30 minutes.

3 Heat the oil and half of the butter together in a large frying pan and gently fry the escalopes, one at a time, over a gentle to medium heat for 3–4 minutes on each side. Be aware that too much heat will cause the veal to toughen. Keep the escalopes warm while you cook the remainder.

4 Top each escalope with one-quarter of the remaining butter. Garnish with chives and a sprinkling of paprika. Serve with lemon wedges and buttered tagliatelle, with a green salad or vegetable, if you like.

--- COOK'S TIP ---

To prevent the breadcrumb coating from cracking during cooking, use the back of a knife and lightly form a criss-cross pattern.

Romanian Kebab

Kebabs are popular world-wide, in great part because they are so easily adapted to suit everyone's taste. In this modern version, lean lamb is marinated then grilled with chunks of vegetables to produce a delicious, colourful and healthy meal. Traditionally, an unfermented grape juice (*mustarii*) and local bread is served with the meal.

INGREDIENTS

Serves 6

675g/1½ lb lean lamb, cut into
    4cm/1½ in cubes
12 shallots or button onions
2 green peppers, seeded and cut into
    12 pieces
12 small tomatoes
12 small mushrooms
sprigs of rosemary, to garnish
lemon slices, freshly cooked rice and
    crusty bread, to serve

For the marinade

juice of 1 lemon
120ml/4fl oz/½ cup red wine
1 onion, finely chopped
60ml/4 tbsp olive oil
2.5ml/½ tsp each dried sage
    and rosemary
salt and freshly ground black pepper

1 For the marinade, combine the lemon juice, red wine, onion, olive oil, herbs and seasoning in a bowl.

2 Stir the cubes of lamb into the marinade. Cover and refrigerate for 2–12 hours, stirring occasionally.

3 Remove the lamb from the marinade and thread the pieces on to 6 skewers alternating with the onions, peppers, tomatoes and mushrooms.

COOK'S TIP

To vary this recipe sprinkle over 30ml/ 2 tbsp chopped fresh parsley and finely chopped onion, to garnish.

4 Cook the kebabs over the hot coals of a barbecue or under a preheated grill for 10–15 minutes, turning them once. Use the leftover marinade to brush over the kebabs during cooking to prevent the meat drying out.

5 Serve the kebabs on a bed of freshly cooked rice, sprinkled with fresh rosemary and accompanied by lemon slices and slices of crusty bread.

Chicken with Beans

This substantial Bulgarian casserole is bursting with flavour, texture and colour.

INGREDIENTS

Serves 4–6
275g/10oz dried kidney or other
  beans, soaked overnight
8–12 chicken portions, such as thighs
  and drumsticks
12 bacon rashers, rinded
2 large onions, thinly sliced
250ml/8fl oz/1 cup dry white wine
2.5ml/½ tsp chopped fresh sage
  or oregano
2.5ml/½ tsp chopped fresh rosemary
generous pinch of nutmeg
150ml/¼ pint/⅔ cup soured cream
15ml/1 tbsp chilli powder or paprika
salt and freshly ground black pepper
sprigs of rosemary, to garnish
lemon wedges, to serve

1 Preheat the oven to 180°C/350°F/ Gas 4. Cook the beans in fast-boiling water for 20 minutes. Rinse and drain the beans well and trim the chicken pieces. Season the chicken with salt and pepper.

2 Arrange the bacon around the sides and base of an ovenproof dish. Sprinkle over half of the onion and then half the beans, followed by another layer of onion and then the remaining beans.

3 In a bowl combine the wine with half the fresh sage or oregano, rosemary and nutmeg. Pour over the onion and beans. In another bowl mix together the soured cream and the chilli powder or paprika.

4 Toss the chicken in the soured cream mixture and place on top of the beans. Cover with foil and bake for 1¼–1½ hours, removing the foil for the last 15 minutes of cooking. Serve garnished with rosemary and lemon.

Potted Chicken

This is a traditional Bulgarian way of cooking chicken – in a flameproof pot, on top of the stove – so that it cooks slowly and evenly in its own juices.

INGREDIENTS

Serves 6–8
8 chicken portions
6–8 firm ripe tomatoes, chopped
2 garlic cloves, crushed
3 onions, chopped
60ml/4 tbsp oil or melted lard
250ml/8fl oz/1 cup good chicken stock
2 bay leaves
10ml/2 tsp paprika
10 white peppercorns, bruised
handful of parsley, stalks reserved and
  leaves finely chopped
salt

1 Put the chicken, tomatoes and garlic in the flameproof pot. Cover and cook gently for 10–15 minutes.

——— COOK'S TIP ———

For extra flavour add 1 finely seeded chopped chilli pepper at Step 2.

2 Add the remaining ingredients, except the parsley leaves. Stir well.

3 Cover tightly and cook over a very low heat, stirring occasionally, for about 1¾–2 hours, or until the chicken is tender. Five minutes before the end of cooking, stir in the finely chopped parsley leaves.

Varna-style Chicken

In this tasty dish, the chicken is smothered in a rich, herby sauce.

INGREDIENTS

Serves 8
1.75kg/4lb chicken, cut into 8 pieces
1.5ml/½ tsp chopped fresh thyme
40g/1½oz/3 tbsp butter
45ml/3 tbsp vegetable oil
3–4 garlic cloves, crushed
2 onions, finely chopped
salt and freshly ground white pepper
basil and thyme leaves, to garnish
freshly cooked rice, to serve

For the sauce
120ml/4fl oz/½ cup dry sherry
45ml/3 tbsp tomato purée
a few fresh basil leaves
30ml/2 tbsp white wine vinegar
generous pinch of granulated sugar
5ml/1 tsp mild mustard
400g/14oz can chopped tomatoes
225g/8oz/3 cups mushrooms, sliced

1 Preheat the oven to 180°C/350°F/ Gas 4. Season the chicken with salt, pepper and thyme. In a large frying pan cook the chicken in the butter and oil, until golden brown. Remove from the frying pan, place in an ovenproof dish and keep hot.

COOK'S TIP

Replace the cultivated mushrooms with wild mushrooms, if liked, but do make sure they are cleaned thoroughly before using.

2 Add the garlic and onion to the frying pan and cook for about 2–3 minutes, or until just soft.

3 For the sauce, mix together the sherry, tomato purée, salt and pepper, basil, vinegar and sugar. Add the mustard and tomatoes. Pour into the frying pan and bring to the boil.

4 Reduce the heat and add the mushrooms. Adjust the seasoning with more sugar or vinegar to taste.

5 Pour the tomato sauce over the chicken. Bake in the oven, covered, for 45–60 minutes, or until cooked thoroughly. Serve on a bed of rice, garnished with basil and thyme.

Chicken Ghiveci

Romanians traditionally use a great variety of colourful seasonal vegetables in this hearty stew. A selection of home-grown herbs such as rosemary, marjoram and thyme, would also be added to flavour the stew.

INGREDIENTS

Serves 6

60ml/4 tbsp vegetable oil or
    melted lard
1 mild onion, thinly sliced
2 garlic cloves, crushed
2 red peppers, seeded and sliced
about 1.5kg/3½ lb chicken
90ml/6 tbsp tomato purée
3 potatoes, diced
5ml/1 tsp chopped fresh rosemary
5ml/1 tsp chopped fresh marjoram
5ml/1 tsp chopped fresh thyme
3 carrots, cut into chunks
½ small celeriac, cut into chunks
120ml/4fl oz/½ cup dry white wine
2 courgettes, sliced
salt and freshly ground black pepper
chopped fresh rosemary and
    marjoram, to garnish
dark rye bread, to serve

1 Heat the oil in a large flameproof casserole. Add the onion and garlic and cook for 1–2 minutes until soft; then add the red peppers.

2 Joint the chicken into 6 pieces, place in the casserole and brown gently on all sides.

3 After about 15 minutes add the tomato purée, potatoes, herbs, carrots, celeriac and white wine, and season to taste with salt and pepper. Cook over a gentle heat, covered, for a further 40–50 minutes.

4 Add the courgette slices 5 minutes before the end of cooking. Adjust the seasoning to taste. Garnish with the herbs and serve with dark rye bread.

—————— COOK'S TIP ——————

If fresh herbs are unavailable, replace them with 2.5ml/½ tsp dried herbs.

Duckling Jubilee

This classic dish tastes delicious, and is very easily prepared.

INGREDIENTS

Serves 4

1.75kg/4½lb duckling
60ml/4 tbsp chopped fresh parsley
1 lemon, quartered
3 carrots, sliced
2 celery sticks, sliced
1 onion, roughly chopped
salt and freshly ground black pepper
apricots and sage flowers, to garnish

For the sauce

425g/15oz can apricots in syrup
50g/2oz/¼ cup granulated sugar
10ml/2 tsp English mustard
60ml/4 tbsp apricot jam
15ml/1 tbsp lemon juice
10ml/2 tsp freshly grated lemon rind
50ml/2fl oz/¼ cup fresh orange juice
1.5ml/¼ tsp each ginger and coriander
60–75ml/4–5 tbsp brandy

1 Preheat the oven to 220°C/425°F/ Gas 7. Clean the duck well and pat dry with kitchen paper. Season the skin liberally.

2 Mix together the chopped parsley, lemon, carrots, celery sticks and onion in a bowl, then carefully spoon this into the cavity of the duck.

3 Cook the duck for 45 minutes on a trivet set over a roasting tin. Baste the duck occasionally with its juices.

4 Remove the duck from the oven and prick the skin well. Return it to the oven, reduce the temperature to 180°C/350°F/Gas 4, and cook for a further 1–1½ hours or until the duck is golden brown, tender and crispy.

5 Meanwhile, put the apricots and their syrup, the sugar and mustard in a food processor or blender. Add the jam and process until smooth.

6 Pour the apricot mixture into a pan and stir in the lemon juice and rind, orange juice and spices. Bring to the boil, add the brandy and cook for a further 1–2 minutes. Remove from the heat and adjust the seasoning.

7 Discard the fruit, vegetables and herbs from inside the duck and arrange the bird on a serving platter. Garnish with fresh apricots and sage flowers. Serve the sauce separately.

> —— COOK'S TIP ——
>
> If using a frozen duck, make sure it is thoroughly thawed before cooking.

Turkey Zador with Mlinces

A Croatian recipe for special occasion, the unusual *mlinces*, are used to soak up the juices.

INGREDIENTS

Serves 10–12
about 3kg/7lb turkey, well thawed
   if frozen
2 garlic cloves, halved
115g/4oz smoked bacon,
   finely chopped
30ml/2 tbsp chopped fresh rosemary
120ml/4fl oz/½ cup olive oil
250ml/8fl oz/1 cup dry white wine
grilled bacon, to serve
sprigs of rosemary, to garnish

For the *mlinces*
350g/12oz/3 cups plain flour, sifted
120–150ml/4–5fl oz/½–²⁄₃ cup
   warm water
30ml/2 tbsp oil
sea salt

1 Preheat the oven to 200°C/400°F/ Gas 6. Dry the turkey well inside and out using kitchen paper. Rub all over with the halved garlic.

2 Toss the bacon and rosemary together and use to stuff the turkey neck flap. Secure the skin underneath with a cocktail stick. Brush with the oil.

3 Place the turkey in a roasting tin and cover loosely with foil. Cook for 45–50 minutes. Remove the foil and reduce the oven temperature to 160°C/325°F/Gas 3.

4 Baste the turkey with the juices then pour over the white wine. Cook for 1 hour, basting occasionally with the juices. Reduce the temperature to 150°C/300°F/Gas 2, and continue to cook for a further 45 minutes, basting the turkey well.

5 Meanwhile, make the *mlinces* by kneading the flour with a little salt, the water and oil to make a soft but pliable dough. Divide equally into 4.

6 Roll out the dough thinly on a lightly floured surface into 40cm/ 16in circles. Sprinkle with salt. Bake on baking sheets alongside the turkey for 25 minutes until crisp. Crush into pieces about 6–10cm/2½–4in.

7 About 6–8 minutes before the end of the cooking time for the turkey add the *mlinces* to the meat juices alongside the turkey. Serve with grilled bacon, garnished with rosemary.

FISH

The numerous rivers, and the Adriatic and Black Seas that border the region, have traditionally provided an abundance of fish. Though not as well stocked today as they once were, classic Balkan cooking is proof of the wonderful variety of freshwater and ocean fish available from these natural sources. Carp is the predominant fish, but trout, swordfish and octopus are all popular. Many of these recipes rely on little more than herbs and spices, fresh vegetables or the local grain, mamaliga, to create quick, healthy and tasty meals.

Fish Baked in a Dough Jacket

In this traditional rural recipe, the whole fish is encased in a yeast-based dough, which traps all the juices and flavour.

INGREDIENTS

Serves 4–6
about 1kg/2¼lb whole fish, such as
  grey mullet, skinned and cleaned
flaked sea salt
sprigs of fennel, to garnish
lemon wedges and courgette and dill
  salad, to serve

For the dough
225g/8oz/2 cups strong white
  flour, sifted
1.5ml/¼ tsp salt
7g/¼oz sachet easy-blend dried yeast
1 egg, beaten
100–120ml/3½–4fl oz/⅓–½ cup milk
  and warm water combined

1 Preheat the oven to 180°C/350°F/ Gas 4. Pat the fish dry with kitchen paper and sprinkle inside and out with salt. Cover and chill the fish until the dough is ready for use.

2 Put the flour and salt into a large mixing bowl and stir in the yeast evenly. Make a well in the centre. Whisk together the egg, milk and water, then pour half into the centre of the flour. Knead to make a soft dough.

3 Knead the dough until smooth on a very lightly floured surface. Divide the dough into 2, making one portion slightly larger than the other.

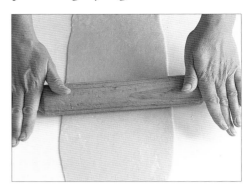

4 Carefully roll out the smaller piece of dough on a lightly floured surface to the shape of your fish, allowing a 5cm/2in border. Lay the dough on a large greased shallow baking sheet. Place the fish on top.

5 Roll out the remaining piece of dough until large enough to cover the fish, again allowing for a 5cm/2in border. Brush the edges of the pastry with water and seal well. Make criss-cross patterns across the top, using a sharp knife. Leave to rise for 30 minutes.

6 Glaze the dough with the remaining egg mixture. Make a small hole in the top of the pastry to allow steam to escape. Bake the fish for 25–30 minutes or until golden brown and well risen. Garnish with sprigs of fennel and serve with wedges of lemon and a salad of finely sliced courgette, tossed in melted butter and sprinkled with dill seeds.

Swordfish Kebabs

Swordfish is a large ocean species found in Balkan waters, the Adriatic and the Black Seas. The firm, meaty flesh is ideal for charcoal grilling, poaching, steaming and baking.

INGREDIENTS

Serves 4

900g/2lb swordfish, skinned
5ml/1 tsp paprika, plus extra
   to garnish
60ml/4 tbsp lemon juice
45ml/3 tbsp olive oil
6 fresh bay leaves
4 small tomatoes
2 green peppers, seeded and cut into
   5cm/2in pieces
2 onions, cut into 4 wedges each
salt and freshly ground white pepper
extra bay leaves, to garnish
lettuce leaves, soured cream, cucumber
   salad and lime or lemon wedges,
   to serve

For the sauce

120ml/4fl oz/½ cup virgin olive oil
juice of 1 lemon
60ml/4 tbsp finely chopped
   fresh parsley
salt and freshly ground black pepper

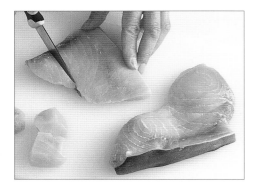

1 Cut the swordfish into 5cm/2in cubes and place in a shallow dish.

2 Mix together the paprika, lemon juice, olive oil and seasoning and pour over the fish. Crush 2 bay leaves over the fish. Leave, covered, in the refrigerator for at least 2 hours.

3 Carefully turn the fish cubes in the marinade once or twice.

4 Thread the fish and vegetables on 4 large skewers; finish with a bay leaf.

5 Cook under a preheated grill or over the hot coals of a barbecue, basting with any remaining marinade mixture from time to time. Turn the fish once during cooking.

6 Meanwhile, for the sauce, in a bowl whisk the oil, lemon juice, parsley and seasoning together until emulsified (thickened) and pour into a jug. Arrange the kebabs on lettuce leaves and serve with the parsley oil sauce, soured cream sprinkled with paprika, a cucumber salad and lime or lemon wedges and garnish with extra bay leaves, if liked.

COOK'S TIP

To help prevent the onion from falling apart during the cooking, keep the root end intact when preparing the onion, so when you slice into it the root will hold the pieces together. Replace the swordfish with sturgeon, halibut or cod, if preferred.

Trout on a Grill

These days, rainbow trout is largely a farmed fish, though it naturally dwells in the rivers, streams and lakes of the Balkans. Its pretty pink flesh and strong flavour encourages a very simple approach, like this one, when it comes to cooking it.

INGREDIENTS

Serves 4
50g/2oz/4 tbsp butter, melted
5ml/1 tsp chopped fresh dill
5ml/1 tsp chopped fresh flat
  leaf parsley
4 trout fillets
45–60ml/3–4 tbsp lemon juice
salt and freshly ground black pepper
baby red Swiss chard leaves and sprigs
  of flat leaf parsley, to garnish

1 Stir together the butter, dill, flat leaf parsley and seasoning.

— COOK'S TIP —

If using a barbecue, put the fish in a double-sided, hinged basket, which allows you to turn the fish over easily. To prevent the head and tail from burning, brush with a little water then dip in granular salt.

2 Brush both sides of the fish with the herb butter before placing it under a preheated grill.

3 Grill for 5 minutes, then carefully turn over and cook the other side, basting with the remaining butter.

4 Just before serving, sprinkle over the lemon juice. Garnish with Swiss chard and sprigs of herbs.

Fish Parcels

Fish cooked in a parcel is a traditional method used by fishermen when cooking their lunch. They used to tie leaves or paper around the catch, dampen the parcel with water, bury it in hot ashes and cover it with a layer of hot coals.

INGREDIENTS

Serves 4
4 small seabass or trout, about
  400g/14oz each
juice of 1 lemon
50g/2oz/4 tbsp butter, melted
a few sprigs of parsley or dill
1/2 fennel bulb, cut into strips
salt and freshly ground black pepper or
  cayenne pepper
cornbread and tomato and cucumber
  salad, to serve

1 Preheat the oven to 180°C/350°F/ Gas 4, or light the barbecue. Remove the head, tail, fins and scales from the fish. Pat dry and season well. Sprinkle with lemon juice.

2 Cut out a double layer of greaseproof or parchment paper, large enough to put the fish into with enough extra to make a good seal. Brush the fish with the melted butter and place it in the centre. Sprinkle with half the parsley or dill and the fennel.

3 Wrap up the fish loosely to make a neat parcel. Press down the edges securely. Bake in the oven for about 15–20 minutes, depending on the thickness of the fish, or for 20–30 minutes if cooking on a barbecue.

4 Transfer the fish to serving plates and peel back the paper when ready to serve. Garnish with the remaining herbs and serve with slices of cornbread and a tomato and cucumber salad.

Onion and Fish Casserole

Choose a firm, white fish, such as cod or grey mullet, for this dish.

INGREDIENTS

Serves 4
45ml/3 tbsp olive oil
4 onions, finely chopped
5ml/1 tsp sea salt
45ml/3 tbsp water
3 garlic cloves, crushed
1 bay leaf
6 allspice berries
2.5ml/½ tsp paprika
4 plum tomatoes, seeded and diced
120ml/4fl oz/½ cup dry white wine,
  plus 45ml/3 tbsp
4 skinless fish steaks, about 175g/
  6oz each
lemon juice, for sprinkling
8 lemon slices
salt and freshly ground black pepper
15ml/1 tbsp chopped fresh parsley,
  to garnish
crusty bread, to serve

1 Preheat the oven to 180°C/350°F/ Gas 4. Put the oil, onion, sea salt and water in a heavy-based pan. Stir well and cook gently, covered, over a very low heat for 45 minutes but do not allow the onion to brown.

— COOK'S TIP —

For extra flavour, if you have time, marinate the fish in the salt, pepper and lemon juice for 1–2 hours in a covered, non-metallic bowl before cooking.

2 Stir in the garlic and cook for 1 minute before adding the bay leaf, allspice, paprika, tomatoes, the 120ml/4fl oz/½ cup wine and seasoning. Cook for 10–15 minutes, stirring occasionally to prevent sticking. Remove and discard the allspice and bay leaf.

3 Spoon a layer of the onion mixture into the base of a shallow ovenproof dish and top with the fish steaks. Sprinkle with a little lemon juice and seasoning.

4 Sprinkle over the remaining white wine and place two lemon slices overlapping on top of each fish steak. Spoon the remaining onion sauce over the fish.

5 Bake the casserole in the oven for 15–20 minutes, or until the sauce thickens and the fish flakes easily. Garnish with a sprinkling of parsley and serve with crusty bread.

Poached Carp with Caraway Seeds

Carp is a favourite freshwater fish in the Balkans as in central Europe; not only is it plentiful but it is also easy to cook. This oil-rich fish dwells in the lakes and rivers and is generally sold alive in the local markets. Choose carp weighing 1.5–1.75kg/3–4lb, otherwise the fish tends to be coarse.

INGREDIENTS

Serves 4
4 carp fillets, about 175–200g/
    6–7oz each
15ml/1 tbsp caraway seeds,
    roughly crushed
40g/1½oz/3 tbsp butter
30ml/2 tbsp snipped fresh chives
1 onion, finely sliced
juice of 1 lemon
175ml/6fl oz/¾ cup dry white wine
salt and freshly ground black pepper
dill and mint, to garnish
cornmeal porridge and green beans,
    to serve

1 Wipe the fish fillets and pat dry with kitchen paper. Season well and press the roughly crushed caraway seeds into the flesh.

2 Heat half the butter in a large frying pan and stir in half the fresh chives, the onion, lemon juice and dry white wine. Bring to the boil, reduce the heat and gently simmer for about 10–12 minutes.

3 Add the fish and poach gently for about 10 minutes. Carefully remove the fillets with a fish slice and keep them warm on a serving plate.

— COOK'S TIP —

The caraway seeds give the dish a very distinctive flavour, so be liberal with them.

4 Continue cooking the stock to reduce it a little, then whisk in the remaining butter. Adjust the seasoning. Pour the sauce over the fish and top with the remaining chives. Garnish with the herbs and serve with cornmeal porridge and green beans.

Fish Stew and Herby Mash

Use swordfish, sea bream, turbot, tuna or any firm fish with few bones. Serve hot or cold.

INGREDIENTS

Serves 4

45ml/3 tbsp olive oil
1 onion, finely chopped
2 garlic cloves, crushed
30ml/2 tbsp tomato purée
3 plum tomatoes, seeded and chopped
15ml/1 tbsp vinegar
1 bay leaf
15ml/1 tbsp chopped fresh flat
    leaf parsley
600ml/1 pint/2½ cups good
    fish stock
675–900g/1½–2lb mixed fish fillets,
    cut into 10cm/4in cubes
675g/1½lb old potatoes, peeled and
    cut into chunks
30ml/2 tbsp soured cream
salt and freshly ground black pepper
chopped fresh flat leaf parsley, bay
    leaves and grated lemon rind,
    to garnish

1 Heat the olive oil in a large pan, and cook the onion and garlic for 2–3 minutes or until just soft. Add the tomato purée, tomatoes, vinegar, bay leaf and parsley. Stir well before pouring in the fish stock. Bring to the boil.

2 Add the pieces of fish to the pan. Bring to the boil again, then reduce the heat and cook for approximately 30 minutes, stirring occasionally.

3 Meanwhile, place the potatoes in a large pan of lightly salted water. Bring to the boil and cook for 20 minutes. Drain well. Return to the pan, add the soured cream and a little pepper. Mash well with a fork.

4 Season the fish to taste. Serve with mashed potato on individual plates or in bowls. Garnish with the parsley and bay leaves and sprinkle grated lemon rind over the mash.

> ——— COOK'S TIP ———
>
> To make fish stock, place all the bones, trimmings, head and any leftover fish pieces in a large pan; add 1–2 carrots, 1 onion, sprigs of fennel or dill, a few peppercorns and a dash of dry white wine. Cover with cold water, bring to the boil then simmer for 20 minutes. Strain through a fine sieve.

Mackerel in Wine Sauce

Dry white wine makes a good accompaniment to this fish.

INGREDIENTS

Serves 4

4 mackerel, filleted, with tails on
50ml/2fl oz/¼ cup olive oil
2 onions, finely sliced
3 garlic cloves, finely chopped
397g/14oz can plum tomatoes
250ml/8fl oz/1 cup dry white wine
salt and freshly ground black pepper
lemon slices, and parsley, to garnish
crusty rye bread, to serve

1 Preheat the oven to 200°C/400°F/ Gas 6. Pat the fish fillets dry with kitchen paper.

2 In a flameproof casserole heat the oil and cook the onions for 3–4 minutes or until soft. Stir in the garlic and cook for a further 2 minutes.

3 Spoon in the tomatoes and add the seasoning. Cook for 20 minutes.

4 Carefully add two of the mackerel fillets, skin side uppermost. Cook for 5 minutes on one side then remove and keep warm while you cook the remaining two mackerel. Using a fish slice, carefully transfer the four fillets to individual ovenproof dishes, the cooked side uppermost. Fold each fish loosely in half and pour in the tomato sauce, dividing it among the dishes.

5 Pour in the wine and cover each dish with foil. Cook in the oven for a further 25 minutes. Serve garnished with slices of lemon, sprigs of parsley and a little chopped parsley, accompanied by crusty rye bread.

Carp Stuffed with Walnuts

Serve this elaborate dish on 6 December for Saint Nikolas, the patron saint of fishermen.

INGREDIENTS

Serves 10
about 1.5kg/3lb whole carp, scaled, cleaned and roe reserved
coarse sea salt

For the stuffing
175ml/6fl oz/³/₄ cup walnut oil
675g/1½lb onions, finely sliced
5ml/1 tsp paprika
pinch of cinnamon
175g/6oz/1½ cups walnuts, chopped
15ml/1 tbsp chopped fresh parsley
10ml/2 tsp fresh lemon juice
2 tomatoes, sliced
250ml/8fl oz/1 cup tomato juice
salt and freshly ground black pepper
walnuts and fennel sprigs, to garnish

1 Preheat the oven to 180°C/350°F/Gas 4. Sprinkle the inside of the fish with a little sea salt.

2 In a frying pan, heat the oil then cook the onions, paprika and cinnamon together until soft.

3 Remove any membrane or skin from the roe and roughly chop.

4 Add the roe and walnuts to the frying pan and cook, stirring all the time, for 5–6 minutes. Leave to cool before stirring in the parsley and lemon juice. Season to taste.

5 Fill the cavity of the fish with half of the filling and secure with cocktail sticks. Spoon the remaining stuffing into the base of an ovenproof dish and then place the fish on top.

6 Arrange the sliced tomatoes over the top of the fish and spoon over the tomato juice. Bake in the oven for 30–45 minutes, or until the fish is browned and flakes easily.

7 Carefully transfer to a serving plate. Discard the cocktail sticks before serving the fish sprinkled with extra walnut pieces and sprigs of fennel.

Stuffed Red Snapper

There are a number of local flavours combined in this unusual recipe – the red snapper filled with carp, sharpened by the salty cheese and dill pickle.

INGREDIENTS

Serves 4

4 small red snapper, about 450g/1lb
   each, filleted and heads and
   fins removed
juice of 1 lemon
350g/12oz fish fillets, such as carp,
   pike or sole, skinned
1 egg white
2.5ml/½ tsp chopped fresh tarragon
1 dill pickle, sliced
40g/1½oz/¾ cup fresh breadcrumbs
40g/1½oz/¼ cup feta cheese or
   brinza, roughly crumbled
salt and freshly ground white pepper
25g/1oz/2 tbsp butter, melted
sprigs of tarragon or sweet cicely plus
   pansies or other edible flowers,
   to garnish
lemon wedges, to serve

1 Preheat the oven to 180°C/350°F/ Gas 4. Wipe out the snapper and pat dry, removing any membrane with a little salt. Liberally rub the lemon juice inside the fish.

2 Put the fish fillets in a food processor and process with the egg white, tarragon, dill pickle, bread-crumbs, cheese and a little ground white pepper, until a smooth paste is formed for the stuffing.

3 Using a spoon, fill the fish with the fish fillet mixture and lay them in an ovenproof dish.

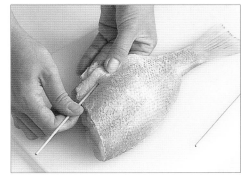

4 Secure the fish with wooden satay sticks and bake for 40–50 minutes. Spoon over the melted butter halfway through cooking.

5 Transfer the fish carefully to a serving plate. Serve with lemon wedges and garnish with fresh sprigs of tarragon or sweet cicely and edible flowers, if liked.

VEGETABLES AND GRAINS

Aubergines, courgettes, capsicum, cucumbers and tomatoes are just some of the vegetables that are available fresh in the Balkan markets. While some of the recipes in this section reflect Italian, Turkish or Greek influences, such as Courgettes with Rice and Stuffed Vine Leaves, others are uniquely Balkan. Mamaliga Baked with Cheese, using the local grain, mamaliga, *is a perfect example of the versatility of this staple ingredient. The excellent* shopska *salads featuring the local yogurt are another typical delight.*

Creamy Aubergine and Mushrooms

This traditional way to serve aubergines may seem unusual to Western cooks, but is based on typical ingredients of the area.

INGREDIENTS

Serves 4–6
2 aubergines
115g/4oz/½ cup unsalted butter
225g/8oz/3 cups mushrooms, sliced
120ml/4fl oz/½ cup good strong
 beef stock
250ml/8fl oz/1 cup double cream
60ml/4 tbsp chopped fresh parsley
salt and freshly ground white pepper
soured cream, to serve (optional)

1 Peel the aubergines with a sharp knife then slice into 7.5cm/3in long sticks, about 5mm/¼ in thick.

2 Put the aubergine on a dish towel and sprinkle liberally with salt.

3 Fold over the dish cloth to cover the aubergine and leave for 30–35 minutes. Use the cloth to squeeze out the moisture from the aubergine.

4 Heat the butter in a large frying pan and cook the aubergine and mushrooms for 10 minutes. Pour in the beef stock and simmer for a further 15 minutes, stirring occasionally.

5 Season to taste before stirring in the cream. Reheat but do not allow to boil. Add 45ml/3 tbsp of the parsley and stir well. Spoon into a warm serving dish and garnish with the remaining parsley. Serve with soured cream, if liked.

COOK'S TIP

For a really smooth vegetable dish, carefully blend together the aubergine and mushrooms in a food processor or blender after the initial 10 minutes of cooking. Add the beef stock and follow the rest of the recipe.

Courgettes with Rice

This dish bears testimony to the influence of Italy, just on the other side of the Adriatic Sea, on Balkan cuisine.

INGREDIENTS

Serves 4 as a main course
8 as a side dish
1kg/2¼lb small or medium courgettes
60ml/4 tbsp olive oil
3 onions, finely chopped
3 garlic cloves, crushed
5ml/1 tsp chilli powder
397g/14oz can chopped tomatoes
200g/7oz/1 cup risotto or round
   grain rice
600–750ml/1–1¼ pints/2½–3 cups
   vegetable or chicken stock
30ml/2 tbsp chopped fresh parsley
30ml/2 tbsp chopped fresh dill
salt and freshly ground white pepper
sprigs of dill and olives, to garnish
thick natural yogurt, to serve

1 Preheat the oven to 190°C/375°F/ Gas 5. Top and tail the courgettes and slice into large chunks.

2 Heat half the olive oil in a large pan and gently fry the onions and garlic until just soft. Stir in the chilli powder and tomatoes and simmer for about 5–8 minutes before adding the courgettes and salt to taste.

COOK'S TIP

Add extra liquid as necessary, during step 5, to prevent the mixture from sticking.

3 Cook over a gentle to medium heat for 10–15 minutes, before stirring the rice into the pan.

4 Add the stock to the pan, cover and simmer for about 45 minutes or until the rice is tender. Stir the mixture occasionally.

5 Remove from the heat and stir in pepper to taste, parsley and dill. Spoon into an ovenproof dish and bake for about 45 minutes.

6 Halfway through cooking, brush the remaining oil over the courgette mixture. Garnish with the dill and olives. Serve with the yogurt.

Thracian Tomato Casserole

This is a typical recipe from the Thracian region of southern Bulgaria. It is eaten at harvest time during the hottest days of the year.

INGREDIENTS

Serves 4
40ml/2½ tbsp olive oil
45ml/3 tbsp chopped fresh flat
  leaf parsley
1kg/2¼lb firm ripe tomatoes
5ml/1 tsp caster sugar
40g/1½oz/scant 1 cup day-old
  breadcrumbs
2.5ml/½ tsp chilli powder
  or paprika
salt
chopped parsley, to garnish
rye bread, to serve

1 Preheat the oven to 200°C/400°F/ Gas 6. Brush a large baking dish with 15ml/1 tbsp of the oil.

2 Sprinkle the chopped flat leaf parsley over the base of the dish. Cut the tomatoes into even slices, discarding the two end slices of each. Arrange the slices of tomato in the dish so that they overlap slightly. Sprinkle them with a little salt and the caster sugar.

--- VARIATION ---

To vary this recipe, replace half the quantity of tomatoes with 450g/1lb courgettes. Slice the courgettes evenly and arrange alternate slices of courgette and tomato in the dish, overlapping the slices as before.

3 In a mixing bowl, stir together the breadcrumbs, the remaining oil and chilli powder or paprika, then sprinkle over the top of the tomatoes.

4 Bake in the oven for 40–50 minutes, covering with foil if the topping is getting too brown. Serve hot or cold, garnished with chopped parsley and accompanied by rye bread.

Mixed Vegetable Casserole

INGREDIENTS

Serves 4
1 aubergine
115g/4oz/½ cup okra, halved
  lengthways
225g/8oz/2 cups frozen or fresh peas
225g/8oz/1½ cups green beans, cut
  into 2.5cm/1in pieces
4 courgettes, cut into 1cm/½in pieces
2 onions, finely chopped
450g/1lb old potatoes, diced into
  2.5cm/1in pieces
1 red pepper, seeded and sliced
397g/14oz can chopped tomatoes
150ml/¼ pint/⅔ cup vegetable stock
60ml/4 tbsp olive oil
75ml/5 tbsp chopped fresh parsley
5ml/1 tsp paprika
salt

For the topping
3 tomatoes, sliced
1 courgette, sliced

1 Preheat the oven to 190°C/375°F/ Gas 5. Dice the aubergine into 2.5cm/1in pieces. Add the vegetables to a large ovenproof casserole.

2 Stir in the canned tomatoes, stock, olive oil, parsley, paprika and salt to taste. Stir well.

3 Level the surface of the vegetables and arrange alternate slices of tomatoes and courgette attractively on top.

4 Put the lid on or cover the casserole dish tightly. Cook for 60–70 minutes. Serve either hot or cold with wedges of crusty bread.

Stuffed Vine Leaves

This vegetarian version of the famous Greek dish uses rice, pine nuts and raisins.

INGREDIENTS

Makes about 40
40 fresh vine leaves
60ml/4 tbsp olive oil
lemon wedges and a crisp salad,
    to serve

For the stuffing
150g/5oz/³/₄ cup long grain
    rice, rinsed
2 bunches spring onions,
    finely chopped
40g/1¹/₂ oz/¹/₄ cup pine nuts
25g/1oz/scant ¹/₄ cup seedless raisins
30ml/2 tbsp chopped fresh mint leaves
60ml/4 tbsp chopped fresh parsley
3.5ml/³/₄ tsp freshly ground
    black pepper
salt

1 Using a knife or a pair of scissors, snip out the thick, coarse stems from the vine leaves. Blanch the leaves in a large pan of boiling salted water until they just begin to change colour. Drain and refresh in cold water.

COOK'S TIP

When fresh vine leaves are unavailable, use 2 packets of vine leaves preserved in brine and rinse then drain well before using.

2 Mix all the stuffing ingredients together in a bowl.

3 Open out the vine leaves, ribbed side uppermost. Place a heaped teaspoonful of the stuffing on each.

4 Fold over the two outer edges to prevent the stuffing from falling out, then roll up the vine leaf from the stem end to form a neat roll.

5 Arrange the stuffed vine leaves neatly in a steamer and sprinkle over the olive oil. Cook over steam for 50–60 minutes, or until the rice is completely cooked. Serve with lemon wedges and a salad, either cold as a *meze* or hot as a starter to a meal.

Stuffed Celeriac

Rather odd-looking, celeriac is a root vegetable that resembles an underdeveloped head of celery, and tastes a bit like sweet, nutty celery. It can be boiled in water or stock, and in this Romanian recipe, it is cooked in a mixture of olive oil and lemon-flavoured water, giving it extra zest.

INGREDIENTS

Serves 4

4 small celeriac, about 200–225g/
   7–8oz each
juice of 2 lemons
150ml/¼ pint/⅔ cup extra virgin
   olive oil
lemon wedges and sprigs of flat leaf
   parsley, to garnish

For the stuffing

6 garlic cloves, finely chopped
5ml/1 tsp black peppercorns,
   finely crushed
60–75ml/4–5 tbsp chopped
   fresh parsley
salt

1 Peel the celeriac carefully with a sharp knife and quickly immerse in a bowl of water and the lemon juice until ready to use.

COOK'S TIP

It is necessary to add the lemon juice to the water in order to help prevent the peeled celeriac discolouring.

2 Reserve the lemon water. Very carefully scoop out the flesh of each celeriac, leaving a shell about 2cm/¾in thick, in which to put the filling.

3 Working quickly, chop up the scooped out celeriac flesh and mix with the garlic and peppercorns. Add the parsley and season with salt.

4 Fill the shells with the stuffing and sit them in a large pan, making sure they remain upright throughout cooking. Pour in the olive oil and enough lemon water to come halfway up the celeriac.

5 Simmer very gently until the celeriac are tender and nearly all the cooking liquid has been absorbed. Serve the celeriac hot or cold with their juices, and garnish with lemon wedges and sprigs of parsley.

Mamaliga Baked with Cheese

Mamaliga, the local cornmeal, is first cooked to a porridge-like consistency, then baked with feta and the local cheese, *kashkaval*, to give it a pleasantly sharp taste.

INGREDIENTS

Serves 4–6
130g/4½oz/generous 1 cup
  coarse ground cornmeal
1 litre/1¾ pints/4 cups water
50g/2oz/4 tbsp unsalted butter
350g/12oz/1½ cups feta cheese or
  brinza, drained and crumbled
50g/2oz/½ cup hard *kashkaval* cheese,
  grated, for sprinkling
salt and freshly ground black pepper
grilled bacon and spring onions, sliced
  lengthways, to garnish
tomato sauce, to serve

1 Preheat the oven to 190°C/375°F/ Gas 5. Stirring occasionally, dry fry the cornmeal in a large pan for 3–4 minutes, or until it changes colour. Remove from the heat.

2 Slowly pour in the water and add a little salt. Return the pan to the heat and stir well until the cornmeal thickens a little. Cover, reduce the heat and leave for 25 minutes to cook, stirring often.

3 Remove from the heat when thick enough to cause a wide trail to be left when a wooden spoon is lifted from the mixture. Stir in the butter, feta cheese or *brinza* and season well.

4 Spoon into a 20cm/8in greased springform tin. Bake for 25–30 minutes or until firm. Leave overnight or for 2–3 hours. Serve sprinkled with *kashkaval* cheese, bacon and spring onions, with tomato sauce.

Mamaliga Balls

Popular snack food, the *mamaliga* balls in this recipe contain bite-sized pieces of salami, but chunks of smoked ham or cheese is equally suitable.

INGREDIENTS

Serves 6–8
250g/9oz/generous 2 cups
  fine cornmeal
600ml/1 pint/2½ cups lightly
  salted water
generous knob of butter
115g/4oz/1 cup salami, roughly
  chopped
oil, for deep-fat frying
salt and freshly ground black pepper
pan-fried tomatoes and chopped fresh
  herbs, to serve

1 Stir the cornmeal and water together in a heavy-based saucepan. Bring to the boil and, stirring all the time, cook for 12 minutes, or until suitable for rolling into balls. Stir in the butter and season well.

COOK'S TIP

Mamaliga is available in several grades, from coarse to fine. Coarse stoneground is often the best type for cooking.

2 With lightly floured hands, roll the balls to double the size of a walnut and place the salami in the middle before rolling up.

3 Fry the balls in the oil at 180–190°C/350–375°F, for 2–3 minutes or until golden brown. Drain well on kitchen paper. Serve with pan-fried tomatoes and chopped herbs.

Baked Cabbage

This economical dish uses the whole cabbage, including the core where much flavour resides.

INGREDIENTS

Serves 4
1 green or white cabbage, about
    675g/1½ lb
15ml/1 tbsp light olive oil
30ml/2 tbsp water
45–60ml/3–4 tbsp vegetable stock
4 firm, ripe tomatoes, peeled
    and chopped
5ml/1 tsp mild chilli powder
salt
15ml/1 tbsp chopped fresh parsley or
    fennel, to garnish, optional

For the topping
3 firm ripe tomatoes, thinly sliced
15ml/1 tbsp olive oil
salt and freshly ground black pepper

1 Preheat the oven to 180°C/350°F/ Gas 4. Finely shred the leaves and the core of the cabbage. Heat the oil in a frying pan with the water and add the cabbage. Cook over a very low heat, to allow the cabbage to sweat, for about 5–10 minutes with the lid on. Stir occasionally.

2 Add the stock and stir in the tomatoes. Cook for a further 10 minutes. Season with the chilli powder and a little salt.

3 Tip the cabbage mixture into the base of an ovenproof dish. Level the surface of the cabbage and arrange the sliced tomatoes on top. Season and brush with the oil to prevent them drying out. Cook for 30–40 minutes, or until the tomatoes are just starting to brown. Serve hot, garnished with a little parsley or fennel sprinkled over the top, if liked.

---- COOK'S TIPS ----

To vary the taste, add seeded, diced red or green peppers to the cabbage with the tomatoes. If you have a shallow flameproof casserole, you could cook the cabbage in it on the hob and then simply transfer the casserole to the oven for baking.

Creamed Courgettes

Like aubergines, courgettes are another versatile vegetable. For extra texture and crunch the courgette in this recipe is covered in a light sprinkling of breadcrumbs before grilling.

INGREDIENTS

Serves 4–6
6 courgettes, about 200g/7oz each
65g/2½oz/5 tbsp unsalted butter
1 onion, finely chopped
60ml/4 tbsp day-old breadcrumbs
salt
olives, lemon slices and sprig of
    parsley, to garnish

1 Trim the courgettes and cut into 1cm/½in slices. Add to a pan of boiling water and cook for 5–8 minutes, or until just tender. Drain very well.

2 Using a potato masher, mash the courgettes or blend in a food processor or blender until smooth.

3 Melt 40g/1½oz/3 tbsp of the butter in a frying pan and cook the onion until soft, then stir in the puréed courgettes. Cook without browning for a further 2–3 minutes, before spooning into a warm ovenproof serving dish.

4 Dot the courgette with the remaining butter and sprinkle over the breadcrumbs. Cook under a preheated grill until golden brown. Garnish with olives, lemon slices and a sprig of parsley just before serving.

COOK'S TIP

As an alternative, replace the courgettes with two large marrows that have been peeled, seeded and diced.

Cucumber and Tomato Salad

This Bulgarian *shopska* salad uses the excellent local yogurt. It is claimed that yogurt originated in Bulgaria. If unavailable, use a Greek-style yogurt instead.

INGREDIENTS

Serves 4
450g/1lb firm ripe tomatoes
½ cucumber
1 onion

For the dressing
60ml/4 tbsp olive or vegetable oil
90ml/6 tbsp thick Greek-style yogurt
30ml/2 tbsp chopped fresh parsley
   or chives
2.5ml/½ tsp vinegar
salt and freshly ground black pepper
1 small hot chilli, seeded and chopped,
   or 2.5cm/1in lengths of chives,
   to garnish
country bread, to serve

1 Skin the tomatoes by first cutting a cross in the base of each tomato. Place in a bowl and cover with boiling water for 1–2 minutes, or until the skin starts to split, then drain and plunge into cold water. Cut the tomatoes into quarters, seed and chop.

2 Chop the cucumber and onion into pieces the same size as the tomatoes and put them all in a bowl.

3 Mix all the dressing ingredients together and season to taste. Pour over the salad and toss all the ingredients together. Sprinkle over black pepper and the chopped chilli or chives to garnish and serve with crusty bread.

Black Olive and Sardine Salad

The combined ingredients – sardines, olives, tomatoes and wine vinegar – bring a real burst of flavour to a delightful light summer salad.

INGREDIENTS

Serves 6
8 large firm ripe tomatoes
1 large red onion
60ml/4 tbsp wine vinegar
90ml/6 tbsp good olive oil
18–24 small sardines, cooked
75g/3oz/¾ cup black pitted olives,
   drained well
salt and freshly ground black pepper
45ml/3 tbsp chopped fresh parsley,
   to garnish

1 Slice the tomatoes into 5mm/¼ in slices. Slice the onion thinly.

2 Arrange the tomatoes on a serving plate, overlapping the slices, then top with the red onion.

3 Mix together the wine vinegar, olive oil and seasoning and spoon over the tomatoes.

4 Top with the sardines and black olives and sprinkle the chopped parsley over the top.

--- COOK'S TIP ---

This recipe works equally well if the sardines are replaced with 6 shelled and halved hard-boiled eggs.

DESSERTS AND BAKES

There is a wonderful choice of puddings and desserts within the Balkan countries, ranging from simple Baked Peaches with cream to rich chocolate tortes, such as Torte Varazdin. Fresh fruit and nuts, such as walnuts and chestnuts, are popular ingredients and are often combined with sugar or honey to make sweet pastry desserts. However, locally produced rose petals and rose water – simply served swirled through a rice pudding for example – are perhaps the most distinctive addition to Balkan desserts.

Walnut and Coffee Slice

This two-layered slice has a rich walnut base and a creamy light coffee topping. Serve with a complementary drink such as a sour cherry liqueur.

INGREDIENTS

Serves 8–12
4 sheets of filo pastry
50g/2oz/4 tbsp unsalted butter, melted
4 eggs, separated
175g/6oz/scant 1 cup caster sugar
90g/3½oz/scant 1 cup walnuts,
   finely ground
walnut pieces and sifted icing sugar,
   to decorate

For the topping
200g/7oz/scant 1 cup unsalted butter,
   at room temperature
1 egg yolk
150g/5oz/¾ cup caster sugar
45ml/3 tbsp cold strong coffee

1 Preheat the oven to 180°C/350°F/ Gas 4. Grease and line a deep 20cm/8in square cake tin. Brush the sheets of filo pastry with the butter, fold them over and place in the base of the prepared tin.

— COOK'S TIPS —

Please note this recipe contains raw egg yolk. Use pistachios in place of the walnuts if preferred, grinding them in a processor.

2 Whisk the egg yolks and sugar in a mixing bowl until thick and pale, and the whisk leaves a trail.

3 Whisk the egg whites until stiff. Fold in the ground nuts.

4 Fold the egg white into the egg yolk mixture. Spoon into the prepared tin. Bake for about 25–30 minutes, until firm. Allow to cool.

5 Meanwhile, for the topping, cream the ingredients well. Spread on the cake with a round-bladed knife. Scatter over the walnut pieces. Chill for at least 3–4 hours or overnight. Sprinkle with icing sugar and cut into fingers, triangles or squares.

Torte Varazdin

The classic chocolate cake is a favourite world-wide, and appears in many guises. In this version from the former Yugoslavia, it is enhanced with a creamy chestnut filling.

INGREDIENTS

Serves 8–12

225g/8oz/1 cup butter, at
  room temperature
225g/8oz/generous 1 cup caster sugar
200g/7oz plain chocolate, melted
6 eggs, separated
130g/4½oz/generous 1 cup plain
  flour, sifted
chocolate curls, to decorate

For the filling

250ml/8fl oz/1 cup double cream,
  lightly whipped
450g/1lb/1¾ cups canned
  chestnut purée
115g/4oz/generous ½ cup caster sugar

For the topping

150g/5oz/10 tbsp unsalted butter
150g/5oz/1¼ cups icing sugar, sifted
115g/4oz plain chocolate, melted

1 Preheat the oven to 180°C/350°F/ Gas 4. Grease and line the base and sides of a 20–23cm/8–9in round cake tin. Cream the butter and sugar together in a bowl until pale and fluffy. Stir in the melted chocolate and egg yolks. Fold the flour carefully into the chocolate mixture.

2 In a grease-free bowl whisk the egg whites until stiff. Add a spoonful of the egg white to the chocolate mixture to loosen it, then carefully fold in the remainder. Spoon the cake mixture into the prepared tin.

3 Bake the cake for 45–50 minutes, or until firm to the touch and a skewer inserted into the middle comes out clean. Cool on a wire rack. When cold, peel off the lining paper and slice the cake in half horizontally.

4 Meanwhile, gently mix the filling ingredients together in a bowl. Sandwich the two cake halves together firmly with the chestnut filling.

5 In a mixing bowl, cream together the butter and sugar for the topping before stirring in the melted chocolate. Using a dampened knife spread the chocolate topping over the sides and top of the cake. Chill for 60 minutes before serving if possible, decorated with chocolate curls.

Baklava

The origins of this recipe are in Greece and Turkey, but it has been willingly adopted throughout south-eastern Europe. It is a very sweet dessert and black coffee is the perfect accompaniment.

INGREDIENTS

Makes 24 pieces

175g/6oz/³⁄₄ cup butter, melted
400g/14oz packet filo pastry, thawed
    if frozen
30ml/2 tbsp lemon juice
60ml/4 tbsp clear thick honey
50g/2oz/¹⁄₄ cup caster sugar
finely grated rind of 1 lemon
10ml/2 tsp cinnamon
200g/7oz/1³⁄₄ cups blanched
    almonds, chopped
200g/7oz/1³⁄₄ cups walnuts, chopped
75g/3oz/³⁄₄ cup pistachios or
    hazelnuts, chopped
chopped pistachios, to decorate

For the syrup

350g/12oz/1³⁄₄ cups caster sugar
115g/4oz/¹⁄₂ cup clear honey
600ml/1 pint/2¹⁄₂ cups water
2 strips of thinly pared lemon rind

1 Preheat the oven to 160°C/325°F/ Gas 3. Brush the base of a shallow 30 × 20cm/12 × 8in loose-bottomed or Swiss roll tin with a little of the melted butter.

2 Using the tin as a guide cut the sheets of filo pastry with a sharp knife to fit the tin exactly.

3 Place one sheet of pastry in the base of the tin, brush with a little melted butter, then repeat until you have used half of the pastry sheets. Set the remaining pastry aside and cover with a clean dish towel.

4 To make the filling, place the lemon juice, honey and sugar in a pan and heat gently until dissolved. Stir in the lemon rind, cinnamon and chopped nuts. Mix thoroughly.

5 Spread half the filling over the pastry, cover with 3 layers of the filo pastry and butter then spread the remaining filling over the pastry.

6 Finish by using up the remaining sheets of pastry and butter on top, and brush the top of the pastry liberally with butter.

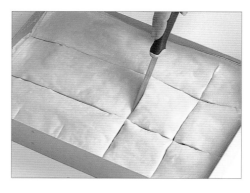

7 Using a sharp knife, carefully mark the pastry into squares, almost cutting through the filling. Bake in the preheated oven for 1 hour, or until crisp and golden brown.

8 Meanwhile, make the syrup. Place the caster sugar, honey, water and lemon rind in a pan and stir over a low heat until the sugar and honey have dissolved. Bring to the boil, then boil for a further 10 minutes until the mixture has thickened slightly.

9 Take the syrup off the heat and leave to cool slightly. Remove the baklava from the oven. Remove and discard the lemon rind from the syrup then pour over the pastry. Leave to soak for 6 hours or overnight. Cut into squares and serve, decorated with chopped pistachios.

Currant Apple Mousse

This Romanian recipe uses locally grown apples and currants, macerated in red wine, to make this creamy mousse.

INGREDIENTS

Serves 4–6
175g/6oz/³/₄ cup currants
175ml/6fl oz/³/₄ cup red wine, plus
    a little extra for topping up
4 crisp eating apples, cored, peeled
    and sliced
250ml/8fl oz/1 cup water
225g/8oz/generous 1 cup
    caster sugar
30ml/2 tbsp cornflour
few drops of pink food
    colouring (optional)
3 egg yolks
5ml/1 tsp vanilla essence
1.5ml/¼ tsp cinnamon
2 egg whites
seedless black grapes, a little caster
    sugar and mint leaves,
    to decorate

1 Soak the currants in the red wine for 1–1½ hours. Drain the currants and set aside. Strain the wine through a fine sieve, to remove most of the currant bits, then top up with more wine as necessary to bring back up to 175ml/6fl oz/³/₄ cup.

2 While the currants are soaking, put the apples in a pan and cook with the water and three-quarters of the caster sugar until soft. Leave to cool.

3 Purée the apples in a processor and then return to the pan.

4 Blend together the cornflour and the red wine and then pour into the apple purée. Cook for about 8–10 minutes, stirring all the time. Add the food colouring, if using.

5 Beat the egg yolks in a bowl with the remaining caster sugar and the vanilla essence until pale and thick.

6 Whisk the apple mixture slowly into the egg yolks. Add the cinnamon and beat until smooth.

7 Refrigerate until thickened. Reserve 5ml/1 tsp of the egg white for decorating and whisk the remainder in a grease-free bowl, until stiff. Fold the currants and the whisked egg whites into the apple mixture and chill well.

8 While the mousse is chilling, make the frosted grapes. Brush the grapes with a little of the reserved egg white and sprinkle with caster sugar. Leave to dry. Use with the mint leaves to decorate the mousse.

Cherry Strudel

There are many varieties of strudel filling in this region, ranging from poppy seed, raisin and honey to sweet cheese. Cherry or apple strudels are among the most popular. A true strudel pastry is very thin, light and crispy, and takes a long time to roll out; nevertheless, it really is worth the effort.

INGREDIENTS

Serves 8–10
250g/9oz/2¼ cups strong flour
75g/3oz/⅔ cup plain flour
1 egg, beaten
150g/5oz/10 tbsp butter, melted
100ml/3½fl oz/½ cup warm water
sifted icing sugar, for dredging

For the filling
65g/2½oz/generous ½ cup walnuts, roughly chopped
115g/4oz/generous ½ cup caster sugar
675g/1½lb cherries, stoned
40g/1½oz/scant 1 cup day-old breadcrumbs

1 Preheat the oven to 200°C/400°F/ Gas 6. Sift the flours together in a warm bowl. Make a well in the centre, add the egg, 115g/4oz/½ cup of the melted butter and the water. Mix to a smooth pliable dough, adding a little extra flour if required. Leave wrapped in clear film for 30 minutes to rest.

2 Meanwhile in a large bowl, mix together the chopped walnuts, sugar, cherries and breadcrumbs.

3 Lay out a clean dish towel and sprinkle it with flour. Carefully roll out the dough until it covers the towel. The dough should be as thin as possible, so that you can see the design on the cloth through it.

4 Dampen the edges with water. Spread the cherry filling over the pastry, leaving a gap all the way round the edge, about 2.5cm/1in wide. Roll up the pastry carefully with the side edges folded in over the filling to prevent it coming out. Use the dish towel to help you roll the pastry.

5 Brush the strudel with the remaining melted butter. Place on a baking sheet and curl into a horseshoe shape. Cook for 30–40 minutes, or until golden brown. Dredge with icing sugar; serve warm or cold.

Boyer Cream

This light and fluffy mousse-like dessert is flavoured with a hint of rose water.

INGREDIENTS

Serves 4–6
225g/8oz/1 cup full-fat cream cheese
75ml/5 tbsp soured cream
2 eggs, separated
50g/2oz/¼ cup vanilla sugar
115g/4oz/²⁄₃ cup raspberries
115g/4oz/1 cup strawberries
sifted icing sugar, to taste
15ml/1 tbsp rose water
halved strawberries, mint leaves and
    small pink roses, to decorate

1 Beat the cream cheese in a bowl with the soured cream and egg yolks until the cheese has softened. Stir in half the sugar.

2 Whisk the egg whites in another bowl until stiff, then whisk in the remaining sugar. Fold the egg whites into the cream cheese mixture. Chill until ready for use.

3 To make the fruit sauce, purée the raspberries and strawberries. Sieve to remove pips; add icing sugar, to taste. Swirl 4–6 glass dishes with a little rose water and divide three-quarters of the sauce between the dishes. Top with the cream cheese mixture. Add the remaining sauce in spoonfuls, swirling it into the cream cheese.

4 Place the dishes on saucers and decorate with halved strawberries, mint leaves and small roses.

Bulgarian Rice Pudding

There are many versions of rice pudding to choose from, but the presence here of pistachios, lemon, cinnamon and rose petals, makes this version a distinctly Bulgarian one.

INGREDIENTS

Serves 4–6
75g/3oz/scant ½ cup short-grain
    or pudding rice
45ml/3 tbsp granulated sugar
900ml/1½ pints/3¾ cups full-
    cream milk
25g/1oz/2 tbsp unsalted butter
1 cinnamon stick
strip of lemon rind
halved pistachios and rose petals,
    to decorate

1 Put the rice, sugar, milk, butter, cinnamon stick and lemon rind into a large double or heavy-based pan.

— COOK'S TIP —

For an extra creamy rice pudding, fold in 150ml/¼ pint/⅔ cup lightly whipped double cream, just before serving.

2 Cook over a very gentle heat, stirring occasionally, for about 1½ hours, or until thick and creamy. Remove and discard the cinnamon stick and lemon rind.

3 Spoon into serving dishes and sprinkle with halved pistachios and rose petals, to decorate.

Lemon Cake

This simple, pleasing Romanian cake is made from a blend of thick yogurt, lemon and honey, with a hint of cinnamon.

INGREDIENTS

Makes 16
50g/2oz/4 tbsp butter, softened
115g/4oz/generous ½ cup caster sugar
2 large eggs, separated
115g/4oz/½ cup Greek yogurt
grated rind of 2 lemons
juice of ½ lemon
150g/5oz/1¼ cups self-raising flour
2.5ml/½ tsp baking powder
curls of lemon rind, to decorate

For the syrup
juice of ½ lemon
60ml/4 tbsp honey
45ml/3 tbsp water
1 small cinnamon stick

1 Preheat the oven to 190°C/375°F/ Gas 5. Grease and line a shallow 18cm/7in square cake tin. Cream together the softened butter and sugar in a bowl until pale and fluffy.

2 Slowly add the egg yolks, Greek yogurt and lemon rind and juice. Beat until smooth. In a separate, grease-free bowl, whisk the egg whites until just stiff.

3 Sift together the flour and baking powder. Fold into the yogurt mixture, then fold in the egg whites.

4 Spoon the mixture into the prepared cake tin. Bake for about 25 minutes, or until golden brown and firm to the touch. Turn out on to a plate and peel off the base paper.

5 Meanwhile, to make the syrup, put the lemon juice, honey, water and cinnamon stick together in a small pan. Stir until boiling then cook until the mixture is syrupy.

6 Remove the pan from the heat. Remove and discard the cinnamon stick. Spoon the warm syrup over the cake, then sprinkle with the lemon rind. Leave to cool completely before cutting into 16 pieces.

— COOK'S TIP —

The local honey has a perfumed flavour due to the pollen collected from the wild plants in the foothills of the fruit orchards. Try and use scented honey in this dish.

Citrus Ricotta Squares

This light cheese cake has a sponge layer top and bottom and a creamy ricotta cheese filling with a hint of citrus.

INGREDIENTS

Makes 16
3 large eggs, separated
175g/6oz/scant 1 cup caster sugar
45ml/3 tbsp hot water
185g/6½ oz/1⅔ cups plain flour, sifted
2.5ml/½ tsp baking powder
icing sugar, sifted, for dredging
long strands of lemon rind,
   to decorate
fresh fruit, to serve

For the filling

500g/1¼ lb/2½ cups ricotta cheese
100ml/3½ fl oz/½ cup double cream,
   lightly whipped
25g/1oz/2 tbsp caster sugar
10ml/2 tsp lemon juice

1 Preheat the oven to 190°C/375°F/ Gas 5. Grease a 30 × 20cm/12 × 8in Swiss roll tin. Whisk together the egg yolks and caster sugar in a large bowl until the mixture is pale and the whisk leaves a trail when lifted. (The mixture should triple in volume.)

COOK'S TIP

An ideal way of serving the citrus ricotta squares is with seasonal soft fruits such as blackberries, peaches or apricots, soaked in a little cherry brandy (*maraska*).

2 Fold the hot water into the egg yolks, together with the flour and baking powder. Lightly whisk the egg whites in a grease-free bowl and then fold these into the egg yolks.

3 Pour the sponge mixture into the prepared tin, tilting it to help ease the mixture into the corners. Bake for 15–20 minutes, or until golden brown and firm to the touch. Turn out and cool on a wire rack, then carefully slice in half horizontally.

4 Make the filling by beating the ricotta cheese in a bowl and then stirring in the cream, caster sugar and lemon juice. Spread the filling on top of the base sponge then top with the remaining sponge half. Press down lightly on the top layer.

5 Chill the cake for 3–4 hours. Just before serving dredge with a little icing sugar and decorate with the lemon rind. Cut into 16 squares and serve with fresh fruit.

Baked Peaches

This Bulgarian recipe uses fresh peaches with a hint of cloves to give an aromatic, spicy flavour. Peaches are plentiful in summer so they are either dried, used in wines or brandy, or bottled to preserve them for use later on.

INGREDIENTS

Serves 6
40g/1½ oz/3 tbsp unsalted butter
6 firm ripe peaches, washed
12 whole cloves
90g/3½oz/½ cup vanilla sugar
45ml/3 tbsp brandy or dry white
    wine (optional)
pistachios, mint leaves and a little sifted
    icing sugar, to decorate
whipped cream, to serve

1 Preheat the oven to 180°C/350°F/ Gas 4. Spread half the butter around an ovenproof dish, making sure both the sides and base are well coated.

2 Halve the peaches and remove the stones. Place the peaches skin side down in the dish. Push a whole clove into the centre of each peach half.

3 Sprinkle with the sugar and dot the remaining butter into each peach half. Drizzle over the brandy or wine, if using. Bake for 30 minutes, or until the peaches are tender.

4 Serve the peaches, hot or cold, with freshly whipped cream, pistachio nuts and sprigs of mint, and sprinkle with a little icing sugar.

Halva

Halva is the name for a sweetmeat or commercial sugar confectionery made throughout the Balkans. It can be based on wheat flour, cornmeal, semolina or rice flour with different proportions of butter, milk, water and sugar. If you are new to *halva*, this is a good basic version to start off with.

INGREDIENTS

Serves 6–8
275g/10oz/1½ cups fine-grained
    semolina
50g/2oz/4 tbsp butter
50g/2oz/¼ cup caster sugar
750ml/1¼ pints/3 cups very hot milk
grated rind of 1 lemon
90g/3½ oz/½ cup walnuts, chopped
chopped walnuts and halved
    pistachios, to decorate
cinnamon, for sprinkling

1 Dry fry the semolina carefully in a very heavy saucepan over a gentle heat for about 5 minutes, stirring continuously, or until the mixture turns a golden colour. Do not let it brown. Remove from the heat and add the butter and sugar, stirring until melted.

COOK'S TIP

Take care when dry frying the semolina so it does not burn on the base of the pan.

2 Return to a low heat and gradually add the milk to the pan, mixing well between each addition. Simmer for 5 minutes, then stir in the lemon rind and walnuts.

3 Simmer for 5 more minutes, stirring all the time, until very thick. Cover and leave for 2–3 minutes.

4 Fluff up the mixture with a fork. Serve warm, decorated with walnuts, pistachios and cinnamon.

Balkan Doughnuts

These flour-based doughnuts are a natural extension of the Eastern European love for dumplings. They are also the ideal showcase for home-made jam and are usually filled with a thick fruity jam, such as cherry, plum or apricot. Ideally, eat the doughnuts on the day of making.

INGREDIENTS

Makes 10–12
225g/8oz/2 cups strong flour, warmed
2.5ml/$\frac{1}{2}$ tsp salt
7g/$\frac{1}{4}$oz sachet easy-blend dried yeast
1 egg, beaten
60–90ml/4–6 tbsp milk
15ml/1 tbsp granulated sugar
about 60ml/4 tbsp cherry jam
oil, for deep-fat frying
50g/2oz/$\frac{1}{4}$ cup caster sugar
2.5ml/$\frac{1}{2}$ tsp cinnamon

1 Sift the flour into a bowl with the salt. Stir in the yeast. Make a well and add the egg, milk and sugar.

2 Mix together well to form a soft dough, adding a little more milk if necessary, to make a smooth, but not sticky, dough.

3 Beat well, cover with clear film and leave for 1–1$\frac{1}{2}$ hours in a warm place to rise until the dough has doubled in size.

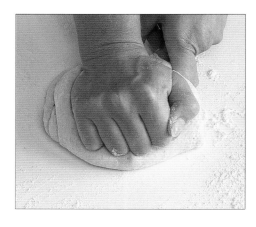

4 Knead the dough on a lightly floured surface and divide it into 10–12 pieces.

5 Shape each into a round and put 5ml/1tsp of jam in the centre.

6 Dampen the edges of the dough with water, then draw them up to form a ball, pressing firmly to ensure that the jam will not escape during cooking. Place on a greased baking sheet and leave to rise for 15 minutes.

7 Heat the oil in a large saucepan to 180°C/350°F, or until a 2.5cm/1in piece of bread turns golden in 60–70 seconds. Fry the doughnuts fairly gently for 5–10 minutes, until golden brown. Drain well on kitchen paper.

8 Mix the caster sugar and cinnamon together on a plate or in a polythene bag and use to liberally coat the doughnuts.

Bird of Paradise Bread

This Bulgarian bread, enriched with eggs and cheese, is named after its traditional decoration.

INGREDIENTS

Serves 10–12
15ml/1 tbsp dried yeast
60ml/4 tbsp lukewarm water
350g/12oz/3 cups flour, sifted
7.5ml/1½ tsp salt
90ml/6 tbsp natural yogurt
5 eggs, beaten
75g/3oz/⅓ cup feta cheese or *brinza*, finely chopped
15ml/1tbsp milk

For the topping
115g/4oz *kashkaval* or Cheddar cheese, sliced into 4 triangles
thick piece of ham, cut into 4 × 2.5cm/1in squares
4 pitted black olives (optional)
about 2.5cm/1in star shape cut out of red pepper

1 Sprinkle the dried yeast over the warm water in a small bowl. Leave to stand for 2–3 minutes, stir well then leave for 5–10 minutes until frothy.

2 Sift the flour and salt into a bowl. Make a well in the centre and pour in the yeast mixture, natural yogurt, 4 of the eggs and the feta cheese or *brinza*. Stir well together to form a dough, adding a little extra flour if necessary. Knead well on a lightly floured surface for about 10 minutes.

3 Shape the dough into an even ball, cover with clear film and leave in a warm place to rise until doubled in size, about 2 hours.

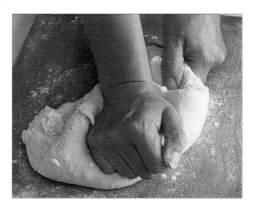

4 On a lightly floured surface gently knead the dough again and shape into a round to fit in a greased 20cm/8in springform tin, or place directly on a lightly buttered baking sheet. In a bowl, beat the 1 remaining egg with the milk and brush liberally over the loaf.

5 To decorate the loaf, arrange the cheese triangles evenly over the top to form a square in the middle. Place the ham and olives, if using, in between the cheese and put the star of red pepper in the centre. Leave to rise for about another 30–45 minutes. Preheat the oven to 200°C/400°F/Gas 6, then bake the loaf for 15 minutes.

6 Reduce the temperature to 180°C/350°F/Gas 4 and cook for a further 30–40 minutes, or until golden brown. Cool on a wire rack.

Mamaliga Bread

Mamaliga, or cornmeal, is one of the basic staple ingredients of the Balkan area. Cheese can be added to this light golden bread to give it a savoury taste.

INGREDIENTS

Makes 1 loaf or 9 small buns
75g/3oz/²/₃ cup self-raising flour
7.5ml/1½ tsp baking powder
75g/3oz/³/₄ cup cornmeal
2.5ml/½ tsp salt
1 egg
150ml/¼ pint/²/₃ cup milk
25g/1oz/¼ cup Cheddar cheese, finely grated (optional)

1 Preheat the oven to 200°C/400°F/ Gas 6. Place the self-raising flour, baking powder, cornmeal and salt into a large mixing bowl. Mix well, then make a well in the centre.

2 Add the egg, milk and Cheddar cheese, if using. Mix well with a wooden spoon.

3 Pour the mixture into a greased 15cm/6in round cake tin or a 9-hole bun tin.

4 Bake for 20–25 minutes or until well risen, golden and firm to the touch. Cool briefly on a wire rack. Serve warm in thick slices.

COOK'S TIP

Cook this loaf immediately after making, otherwise the raising agent will be less effective and the loaf will not be so light.

INDEX

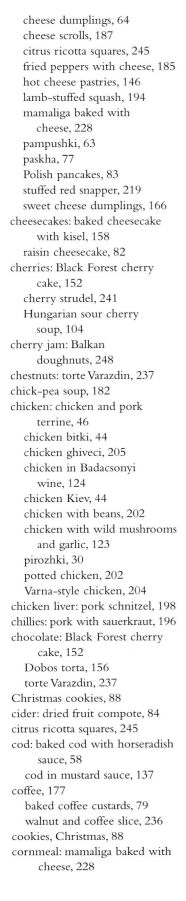

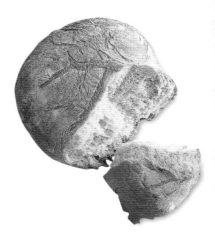